P9-DEV-784

101 Ways to Make Meetings Active

Surefire Ideas to Engage Your Group

Mel Silberman

Assisted by Kathy Clark

Jossey-Bass
Pfeiffer
SAN FRANCISCO

Copyright © 1999 by Jossey-Bass/Pfeiffer

ISBN: 0-7879-4607-9

All rights reserved. No part of this publication may be reproduced, stored in a retrieval system, or transmitted, in any form or by any means, electronic, mechanical, photocopying, recording, or otherwise, without the prior written permission of the publisher.

Printed in the United States of America

Published by

350 Sansome Street, 5th Floor
San Francisco, California 94104-1342
(415) 433-1740; Fax (415) 433-0499
(800) 274-4434; Fax (800) 569-0443

Visit our website at: www.pfeiffer.com

Acquiring Editor: Matthew Holt
Director of Development: Kathleen Dolan Davies
Developmental Editor: Susan Rachmeler
Editor: Rebecca Taff
Senior Production Editor: Dawn Kilgore
Manufacturing Supervisor: Becky Carreño
Interior Design: Gene Crofts
Cover Design: Jennifer Hines

Library of Congress Cataloging-in-Publication Data

Silberman, Melvin L.
    101 ways to make meetings active: surefire ideas to engage your group/
by Mel Silberman: assisted by Kathy Clark.
        p.   cm.
    ISBN 0-7879-4607-9 (acid-free paper).
    1. Business meetings. 2. Meetings. I. Clark, Kathy. 1934-. II. Title. III Title: One hundred one ways to make meetings active. IV. Title: One hundred and one ways to make meetings active.

HF5734.5.S568   1999   99-6095
658.4'56—DC21   CIP

Printing 10 9 8 7 6 5 4 3 2

 This book is printed on acid-free, recycled stock that meets or exceeds the minimum GPO and EPA requirements for recycled paper.

Contents

Preparing Active Meetings   47

Engaging Participants from the Start   87

Stimulating Discussion, Dialogue, and Learning   129

Facilitating Creative Problem Solving   173

Managing Controversy and Conflict   217

Acknowledgments

I have been a facilitator of meetings for over thirty years. During that time, I have been blessed with many opportunities to create, refine, and test the strategies in *101 Ways to Make Meetings Active*. Sometimes, what I've done has bombed or been met with great skepticism—despite its merits. I appreciate all those who helped me through the "school of hard knocks." Other times, I have been successful in guiding meetings of all kinds through challenging waters. I also am grateful for all the votes of confidence I've received from groups that welcomed my facilitation efforts.

No one creates in a vacuum. I have had mentors and colleagues who have given me more creative ideas than one mind can process. Two deserve special mention: Rod Napier and Matti Gershenfeld. Their creative facilitation has been an inspiration to me. Others who have graciously shared their wisdom with me include Rebecca Birch, Sharon Bowman, Cynthia Denton-Ade, Bob Guns, Cathleen Smith Hutchison, Dee Kelsey, Cindy Lindsay, Jana Markowitz, Bill Matthews, Bryan Mattimore, Mary Margaret Palmer, Janis Pasquali, Pam Plumb, and Sivasailam "Thiagi" Thiagarajan.

Karen Lawson has been a vital part of the development and testing of so many of my techniques that this book would not have been possible without her. I also want to thank Liz Clark, Marné Castillo, and Leslie Brunker for their invaluable feedback as I was putting into writing the meeting facilitation ideas in this collection. Once again, my editor, Susan Rachmeler, has helped me hone my writing and organize a book into something that is reader-friendly. Finally, Kathy Clark has done a great job assisting me in this project. She is a talented writer and a really nice person.

During the writing of this book, three people became members of our family: my twin grandsons Noam and Jonah and my daughter-in-law Sara. They join the gang that I rely on the most for encouragement, support, and love: my children, Steven, Lisa, and Gabe, my son-in-law Daniel, and my wife Shoshana.

Introduction

· ·

The immediate reaction of most to an imminent meeting, whether at work or after hours, is a long, drawn-out yawn. Those who have to attend dull meetings are as bored with them as the people who are responsible for conducting them are frustrated. It shouldn't be that way, and it doesn't have to be that way.

"Dull and deadly" is not the way to accomplish things. Active participation is the single most important factor in successful meetings. But, it won't happen if you don't plan for it by using a wide variety of meeting techniques that encourage the highest possible level of active, enthusiastic participation. *101 Ways to Make Meetings Active* offers lots of simple but powerful techniques for pumping energy into your meetings and turning them into uncommonly attractive and effective ways to build teamwork.

101 Ways to Make Meetings Active is a wake-up call that rings for both the board and the bored. To the best of my knowledge, it provides the largest collection of strategies ever published to brighten meetings and move along the action. At the same time, it gets people to do what they're supposed to do—whether it's discussing urgent issues, creating novel ideas, solving tough problems, making important decisions, or planning a successful event or project.

Throughout the book, you will find suggestions for mixing things up at meetings of all kinds and for groups and teams of all sizes. These techniques have a proven track record. They work for small casual gatherings, as well as for more formal events—and even huge throngs. Many work fine for one-time meetings. All of them will benefit groups with multiple session meetings. They also do not require special training to implement. Anyone who might lead a meeting will receive step-by-step instructions on how to proceed with each technique.

The book begins with "The Nuts and Bolts of Active Meetings." In this section, you will find one hundred and forty facilitation tips on how to organize and conduct active meetings. Included are:

- "Ten Layouts for Setting Up a Meeting Room"
- "Ten Ways to Learn New Names"
- "Ten Methods for Obtaining Group Participation"
- "Ten Tips When Facilitating Discussions"
- "Ten Meeting Roles and Responsibilities"
- "Ten Alternatives for Assigning Jobs"
- "Ten Timesavers During Active Meetings"
- "Ten Props to Employ During Active Meetings"
- "Ten Tricks for Calling Participants to Order"
- "Ten Methods to Deal with Difficult Participants"
- "Ten Energizers to Wake Up or Relax a Group"
- "Ten Things to Do When the Group Is Stuck"
- "Ten Tips to Make Flip Charts Graphic"
- "Ten Questions to Process a Meeting"

The 101 strategies described in the book are organized in the following sections:

- "Preparing Active Meetings"
- "Engaging Participants from the Start"
- "Stimulating Discussion, Dialogue, and Learning"
- "Facilitating Creative Problem Solving"
- "Managing Controversy and Conflict"
- "Building Consensus and Commitment"
- "Creating Unforgettable Endings"

Treat *101 Ways to Make Meetings Active* as a cookbook offering enticing recipes to obtain the most out of the time spent—from helping people to walk into the meeting ready to participate, getting the meeting off to a roaring start, and motivating people finally to roll up their sleeves and work hard and smart.

For your convenience in locating a recipe that's right for your group, each strategy is coded as follows:

Group Size:

Time Required:

Activity Tone:

One final word! Use these techniques "as is" or adapt them to fit your needs. And add your own creativity! As you do, bear in mind these suggestions:

- Don't experiment wildly. Try out one method at a time until you and your group gain confidence.

- When you introduce a method to participants, sell it as an alternative to the usual way of doing things that you think might be worth a try. Obtain your group's okay to experiment, and obtain their feedback when you're done.

- Don't overload participants with too many techniques. *Less is often more.* Use just a few to enliven your meetings.

- Make your instructions crystal clear. Demonstrate or illustrate what participants are expected to do so that there is no confusion that might distract them from getting the most out of the technique.

The Nuts and Bolts of Active Meetings

Before attempting to facilitate the 101 active meeting strategies described in this book, you may find it useful to read this section. Many of the strategies utilize the tips you are about to read, which form the "nuts and bolts" of making meeting active.

On the pages that follow, you will find fourteen "top ten" lists, totaling one hundred and forty facilitation tips. You will find ideas on how to build more quality, activity, variety, and direction into your meetings from beginning to end. I have developed the lists to help facilitators identify, at a glance, several choices available to them at different points in the course of conducting a meeting. Many of these ideas are well-known. I hope that having an organized list of them will make your job of being an active meeting facilitator easier.

Ten Layouts for Setting Up a Meeting Room

The physical environment in a meeting space can make or break how active and participatory the meeting will be. No setup is ideal, but there are many options from which to choose. The "interior decorating" of meetings is fun and challenging, especially when the furniture is less than ideal. In some cases, furniture can be easily rearranged to create different setups. If you choose to do so, ask participants to help move tables and chairs. That makes them "active" too.

1. **Conference Tables.** It is best if the table is round or square. This arrangement minimizes the importance of the meeting leader and maximizes the importance of the participants. Each person is equally distant from others and can see the others easily.

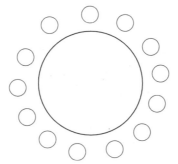 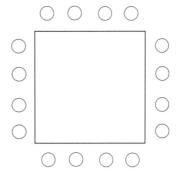

A long rectangular table often creates a sense of formality, especially if the facilitator is at the head of the table. If you only have access to a long, rectangular table, sit in the middle of the wider side.

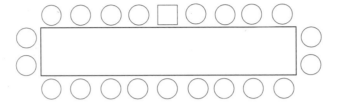

You can form a conference table arrangement by joining together several smaller tables.

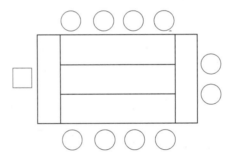

2. **U-Shaped Arrangements.** A U-shape is an all-purpose setup for a meeting in which there are presentations. With this setup, participants have a reading and writing surface, they can see the facilitator and a visual medium easily, and they are in face-to-face contact with one another. It is also easy to pair up participants, especially when there are two seats per table. The arrangement is ideal for distributing handouts quickly too because you can enter the U and walk to different points with sets of materials. You can set up oblong tables in a squared-off U.

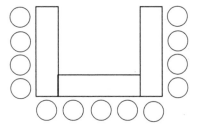

Be sure there is enough perimeter space in the room so that subgroups of three or more participants can pull back from the tables and face one another.

When there are more than sixteen participants, a U can start to resemble a bowling alley or a bridge. It is much better, in this case, to bring all participants in closer contact by seating some participants inside the U, as shown.

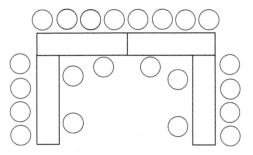

3. **Circles.** Simply seating participants in a circle without tables promotes the most direct face-to-face interaction. A circle is ideal for full-group discussion. Assuming there is enough perimeter space, you can ask participants to arrange their chairs quickly into many subgroup arrangements.

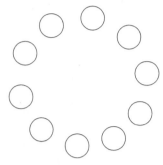

If you want a table surface available for participants, use a peripheral arrangement.

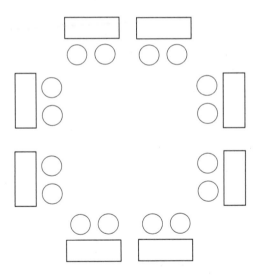

4. **Team Style.** In large meetings, grouping circular or oblong tables around the room enables you to promote team interaction. You can place seats fully around the tables for the most intimate setting. If you do, some participants will have to turn their chairs around to face the front of the room to see you, a flip chart, a blackboard, or a screen.

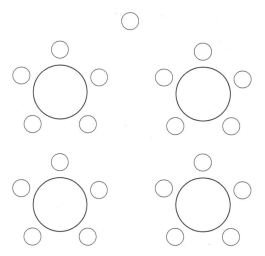

Or you can place seats around the tables so that no participant has his or her back to the front of the room.

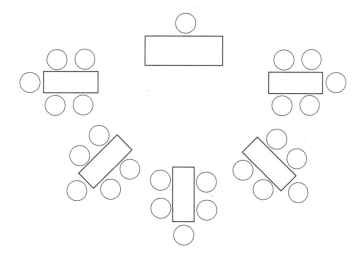

5. **Group on Group.** This arrangement allows you to conduct fishbowl discussions (see "Ten Methods for Obtaining Group Participation" on page 17 and "Three-Stage Fishbowl

Discussion" on page 133). The most typical design is two concentric circles of chairs.

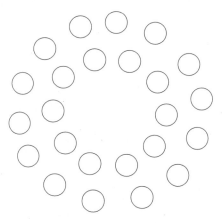

A conference table is ideal for a fishbowl discussion. Designate the participants seated at one side of the table as the discussants. Other participants observe and listen. If you wish, rotate the discussion to a different side of the table.

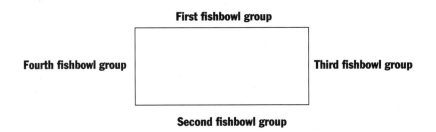

6. **Breakout Groupings.** If the room is large enough or if nearby space is available, arrange (in advance when feasible) tables and/or chairs that subgroups can go to for team-based discussion and problem solving. Keep the breakout settings as far from one another as they can be so that no team is dis-

turbed by the others. However, avoid using breakout spaces that are so far from the main room that the connection to it is difficult to maintain.

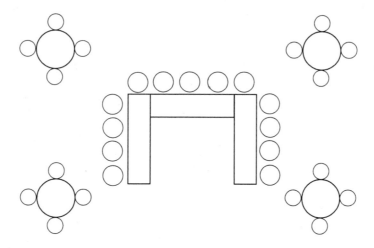

7. **Paired Seating.** This arrangement requires seating (with or without tables or desks) in twos. Everyone is together in one group, but discussion partners are already in place.

8. **Chevron.** A traditional "classroom" setup (rows of tables) is not desirable for active meetings. However, when there are many participants (thirty or more) and only oblong tables are available, it is sometimes necessary to arrange participants classroom style. A repeated V or chevron arrangement, when possible, creates less distance between people and better frontal visibility. It also provides participants with a greater opportunity to see one another than the traditional classroom setup does. In this arrangement, it is best to place aisles off-center.

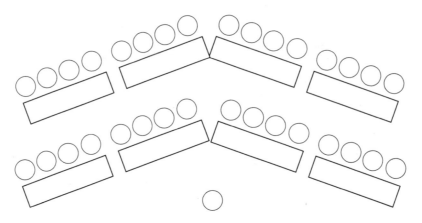

9. **Traditional Classroom.** If you have no choice but to use a series of straight rows of desks or tables and chairs, all is not lost. Group chairs in pairs to allow for the use of discussion partners. Try to create an even number of rows and enough space between them so that pairs of participants in the odd-number rows can turn their chairs around and create a quartet with the pair seated directly behind them.

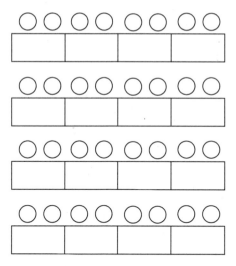

10. **Auditorium.** Although an auditorium is a very limiting environment for active meetings, there is still hope. If the seats are movable, place them in an arc to create greater closeness and to allow participants to see one another better.

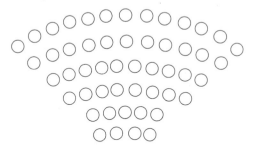

If the seats are fixed, ask participants to seat themselves as close to the center as possible. Be assertive about this request; consider cordoning off sections of the auditorium.

Remember: No matter how large the auditorium and the size of the audience, you can still pair up participants for discussion purposes.

Ten Ways to Learn New Names

In an active meeting environment, it's important that participants be able to call on or refer to one another by name. Beyond name tags or name tents, there are a variety of ways to learn others' names. Some are relatively straightforward; some make learning names into a game.

1. **Name-Learning Assignment.** Ask participants to learn as many names as possible, either by going up to others and introducing themselves or by reading one another's name tags. After several minutes, stop the group and ask the participants to cover up or discard name tags, name lists, and the like. Now, challenge participants to look around and quiz themselves on the names of others in the group. Repeat the learning and self-quizzing activity as many times as you like. Within ten minutes, it should be possible for participants to learn at least twenty names.

2. **Name Chain.** Ask each participant in turn to share his or her name and the names of the people who have already introduced themselves. For example, the first person to introduce himself or herself need only say his or her name, but the second person must give the first person's name as well as his or her own. As the chain becomes longer, there will be more names to remember; however, the names will by then have been repeated several times. You can make the name chain alliterative by inviting each person to use an adjective before

his or her name that begins with the same letter, as in "Creative Carol" or "Lucky Lee." The alliterative adjectives help others to remember the participants' names and often add humor to the activity. Or invite participants to say their names and then accompany them with some physical movement. The movement then becomes a mnemonic aid.

3. **Alphabetical Lineup.** Invite participants to arrange themselves in alphabetical order by their first names. This task forces participants to find out other names in the group. Or do a nonverbal name lineup as a way to review names after participants have introduced themselves in conventional fashion. Ask participants to line up in alphabetical order by their first names *without talking to one another.*

4. **Name Bingo.** Ask participants to mill around the room and meet one another. As they exchange names, have them write each name anywhere on a blank bingo form you have made for them. Create a 3 x 3 format of squares if the group has fewer than ten people, a 4 x 4 format if the group has sixteen or fewer, and a 5 x 5 format if the group has twenty-five or fewer. Instruct participants to place an "O" on any box not used up after meeting each participant. Then place a copy of everyone's name in a hat. As the hat is passed around the group, each participant picks a name out of the hat. Everyone places an "X" on the box on their form containing the name picked. Whenever any player obtains all names horizontally, vertically, or diagonally, he or she yells, "Bingo!" Eventually, everyone will get bingo several times.

5. **Name Tag Mix-Up.** Give each participant the name tag of someone else in the group and ask each person to find the owner of the name tag. Invite participants to circulate until every person receives his or her own name tag.

6. **Alphabetical Sign-In.** Pre-mark twenty-six sheets of flip-chart paper with the letters of the alphabet. Tape the flip-chart paper to walls around the room. Direct participants to

sign the sheet containing the first initial of their name and to find others with the same initial. Then instruct the participants to look over the other sheets and attempt to identify as many names and faces as possible.

7. **Do You Know Your Neighbors?** Form a circle and place one participant in the middle. Ask that person to point to someone in the circle and challenge him or her with the question: "Do you know your neighbors?" If the person in the circle can successfully say the names of the people immediately to his or her right and left, the person in the middle stays there and challenges another person in the circle. When a participant fails the neighbor test, he or she replaces the person in the middle. As the game is played, frequently change the positions of the participants in the circle.

8. **Personalized Name Tags.** Provide materials so that each participant can develop a name tag that uses any of the following:
   - Interesting calligraphy
   - A personal logo
   - A zodiac sign
   - An object or animal that symbolizes some personal quality
   - A coat of arms
   - A collage of magazine cutouts that contain favorite expressions or objects

   Ask participants to meet one another and to learn names.

9. **Name Toss.** Have group members stand in a circle with one person holding an object that can be easily thrown and caught, such as a soft ball or a beanbag. The member holding the object says his or her name and tosses the object to another group member. The person catching the object gives his or her name and tosses the object to another group member. Continue the tossing until all participants have introduced themselves. When the final member has been introduced, ask

that person to say the name of another group member and then toss the object to that person. The receiver than repeats the name of the person who tossed him or her the object and says the name of another group member before tossing the object to that person.

10. **What's in a Name?** Have participants introduce themselves and then share any of the following about their names:

   • What I like or dislike about my name

   • Who I was named after

   • A nickname that I like or dislike

   • The origin of my name

   After these introductions, challenge participants to write down the names of all the members of the group.

Ten Methods for Obtaining Group Participation

Active meetings cannot occur without the involvement of participants. There are a variety of ways to structure discussion and to obtain responses from participants during a meeting. Some methods are especially suitable when time is limited or participation needs to be coaxed. You might also consider combining these methods. For example, you might use subgroup discussion and then invite a spokesperson from each subgroup to serve on a panel.

1. **Open Discussion.** Welcome any comments from anyone in the group. If you are worried that the ensuing discussion might be too lengthy, say beforehand, "We have time for four or five short comments. Who would like to begin?" To encourage several participants to volunteer comments, ask, "How many of you would like to comment on this matter?" Then note who wants to participate and establish an order of participation.

2. **Subgroup Discussion.** Form participants into subgroups of three to six members. Use subgroups when you have sufficient time for discussion. This is one of the key methods for obtaining everyone's participation. Several methods in this book are based on subgroup discussion. Usually, it is desirable to ask each subgroup to summarize its discussion for the

remainder of the groups, but sometimes it is not necessary. Make sure subgroup members are directly facing one another during their discussion.

3. **Partners.** Form participants into pairs and ask them to discuss and problem solve together. Use partners when you want to involve everybody, but do not have enough time for subgroup discussion. A pair is an effective discussion format to enable every participant to talk about an issue prior to whole group discussion. It may be especially helpful with large groups.

4. **Response Cards.** Pass out index cards and request that participants record their comments or ideas on the cards. Use response cards to save time or to provide anonymity for personally threatening self-disclosures. Cards can also be used in brainstorming sessions (see "Brainwriting," on page 183). The cards can be passed around the group, shuffled and redistributed to individual participants, or collected for your reading and review.

5. **Polling**. Design a short survey to fill out and tally on the spot, or verbally poll participants. Use polling to obtain data quickly and in a quantifiable form. If you use a written survey, try to give the results to participants as quickly as possible. If you use a verbal survey, ask for a show of hands or invite participants to hold up answer cards (see "Instant Assessment" on page 157). Polling can be useful in building consensus (see "Polling for Consensus" on page 263).

6. **Go-Arounds.** Invite each participant to contribute a short response to a key question by going around the entire group. Use go-arounds when you want to obtain something quickly from each participant. Sentence stems (for example, "One idea to save costs is. . . .") are useful in conducting go-arounds. Invite participants to pass when they wish. Avoid repetition, if you want, by asking each participant for a new contribution to the process. In large meetings, use go-

arounds for only a portion of the group (for example, all new members).

7. **Calling on the Next Speaker.** Ask participants to raise their hands when they want to share their views and request that the present speaker call on the next speaker (rather than the facilitator doing so). Use this method when you are sure there is a lot of interest in the discussion or activity and you wish to promote participant interaction (see "Town Meeting" on page 131).

8. **Panels**. Invite a small number of participants to present their views in front of the entire group. An informal panel can be created by asking for the views of a designated number of participants who remain in their seats. Use panels when time permits to generate a focused exchange of ideas. Rotate panelists to increase participation.

9. **Fishbowl.** Ask a portion of the group to form a discussion circle, and have the remaining participants form a listening circle around them. Rotate new groups into the inner circle to continue the discussion (see "Three-Stage Fishbowl Discussion" on page 133). Use fishbowls to help bring focus to large-group discussions. Although time-consuming, this is the best method for combining the virtues of large-group and small-group discussion. As a variation to concentric circles, participants can remain seated at tables and you can invite different tables or parts of a table to discuss the topic as the others listen.

10. **Games.** Use an enjoyable activity or a quiz game to elicit participants' ideas, opinions, and knowledge. Games stimulate energy and involvement. There are many collections of games suitable for meetings. You will also find several in this book.

Ten Tips When Facilitating Discussion

During an active meeting, you want lots of group discussion. Your role is to facilitate the flow of comments from participants. Although it is not necessary to interject your comments after each participant speaks, periodically assisting the group with their contributions can be helpful. Here is a ten-point facilitation menu to use as you lead group discussions.

1. **Paraphrase.** Paraphrase what a participant has said so that he or she feels understood and so that the other participants can hear a concise summary of what has been said. Say something like,

   "So, what you're saying is that we need to go slowly in changing our organizational structure."

2. **Check for Meaning.** Check your understanding of a participant's statement or ask the participant to clarify what he or she is saying. Say something like,

   "Are you saying that this plan is not realistic? I'm not sure that I understand exactly what you mean."

3. **Give Positive Feedback.** Compliment an interesting or insightful comment. Say,

   "That's a good point. I'm glad that you brought that to our attention."

4. **Expand.** Elaborate on a participant's contribution to the discussion with examples, or suggest a new way to view the problem. Try,

   "Your comments provide an interesting point from the employee's perspective. It could also be useful to consider how management would view the same situation."

5. **Increase the Pace.** Energize a discussion by quickening the pace, using humor, or, if necessary, prodding the group for more contributions by saying something like,

   "Oh my, we have lots of tired people at this meeting! Here's a challenge for you. For the next two minutes, let's see how many ways we can think of to increase cooperation within our department."

6. **Devil's Advocate.** Disagree (gently) with a participant's comments to stimulate further discussion. For example,

   "I can see where you are coming from, but I'm not sure that what you are describing is always the case. Has anyone else had an experience that is different from Jim's?"

7. **Relieve Tension.** Mediate differences of opinion between participants and relieve any tensions that may be brewing. For instance,

   "I think that Susan and Mary are not really disagreeing with each other, but are just bringing out two different sides of this issue."

8. **Consolidate.** Pull together ideas, showing their relationship to each other, for example,

   "As you can see from Dan's and Jean's comments, we seem to have the resources and commitment to expand our programming."

9. **Change the Process.** Alter the method for obtaining participation or by having the group evaluate ideas that have been presented. Say something like,

   "Let's break into smaller groups and see whether you can come up with some typical customer objections to the products that were covered in the presentation this morning."

10. **Summarize**. Summarize (and record, if desired) the major views of the group, for example,

"I have noted four major reasons that have come from our discussion about why our managers do not delegate enough responsibility to their staff: (1) lack of confidence, (2) fear of failure, (3) comfort in doing the task themselves, and (4) fear of being replaced.

Ten Meeting Roles and Responsibilities

There is a well-known, humorous story of what might happen if each participant is not equally responsible for the group's success.

> *A team had four members named Everybody, Somebody, Anybody, and Nobody. There was an important job to be done. Everybody was sure that Somebody would do it. Anybody could have done it, but Nobody did it. Everybody got angry about that because it was Somebody's job. It ended up that Everybody blamed Somebody when Nobody did what Anybody could have done.*

Meetings can be more effective by giving jobs to several participants to "divide up the labor" and share responsibility. Here are some possible "hats" that people can wear in your meetings. Consider rotating them to include everyone. Too often, certain individuals are pegged for certain jobs.

1. **Facilitator.** This person leads all or a portion of a meeting—providing structure, giving direction, and stimulating and encouraging participation, problem solving, and consensus.

2. **Timekeeper.** This person tells the group how much time is left for a specific agenda item and alerts the group when time limits are being approached.

3. **Minute Taker**. This person takes notes on the meeting discussion, records decisions, and disseminates them as meeting minutes as soon as possible after the meeting.

4. **Record Keeper.** This person maintains all the records accumulated by the group, such as the agenda, minutes, member information, reports, correspondence, data, and other documentation.

5. **Flip-Chart Scribe.** This person records group ideas quickly and legibly on a flip chart or other recording surface.

6. **Researcher.** This person researches information of use to the group.

7. **Energizer.** This person conducts activities to energize or relax the meeting participants.

8. **Meeting Planner.** This person organizes and coordinates all the behind-the-scene details of a meeting session.

9. **Point of Contact.** This person acts as a point of contact for participants between meetings. He or she can also be responsible for maintaining contact with outside parties who may be interested in the group's proceedings.

10. **Process Observer.** This person observes the group process and shares his or her observations with the group when appropriate.

Ten Alternatives for Assigning Jobs

....

As just noted, one of the ways to divide the labor in active meetings is to assign jobs to some of the participants. Often, you can simply ask for volunteers to assume some of these responsibilities. Sometimes, it is fun and efficient to use a creative selection strategy. This may be especially appropriate when you are asking participants to work in small groups or when you want to break down traditional role assignments (for example, a clerical person always taking the notes).

1. **Alphabetical Assignment.** Assign jobs in alphabetical order by first name. In a long-term group, rotate jobs using this order.

2. **Birthday Assignment.** Make assignments in chronological order by participants' birthdays. In a long-term group, rotate jobs using this order.

3. **Number Lottery.** Ask participants to count off. Place pieces of paper with the numbers held by group members in a hat, draw a number, and assign the person with that number to the job.

4. **Card Drawing.** Ask participants to draw playing cards from a deck and assign roles based on such outcomes as the person with the highest or lowest card, high red or black card, high face card, and so forth.

5. **Article of Clothing.** Assign responsibilities by selecting corresponding articles of clothing, such as eye glasses, silver jewelry, a sweater, or brown shoes.

6. **Voting.** Ask group members to vote on the job recipient. One popular method is to tell members to point to the person they are voting for. The person with the most fingers pointing at him or her gets the job.

7. **Random Assignment.** Ask each member to reveal the sum of the last four digits of his or her home phone number (for example, 9999 equals thirty-six). Announce a number from one to thirty-six. Award the job to the person in the group whose sum comes closest to that number.

8. **Pet Lovers.** Assign a designated job to the person with the greatest number of pets.

9. **Family Size.** Assign a designated job to the person with the most (or fewest) siblings.

10. **Door Prize.** Prior to the meeting, place a sticker in such a way as to identity one member per group. You might place a sticker on a name tag or tent, a meeting folder, or on a seat or table surface. The person receiving the sticker gets the "prize" of a specific group job. For awarding more than one job, use stickers of different colors.

Ten Timesavers During Active Meetings

Active meetings take time. Therefore, it is crucial that no time be wasted. The following are some ways to save time:

1. **Start on Time.** This sends a message to latecomers that you are serious. If all of the participants are not yet in the room, begin the meeting, if you wish, with a discussion or filler activity for which complete attendance is not necessary.

2. **Give Clear Instructions**. Do not start a meeting activity when participants are confused about what to do. If the directions are complicated, put them in writing.

3. **Distribute Meeting Materials in Advance.** Prepare documents in packets prior to the session. Distribute packets to key areas of the room so that several people can assist with distribution, or leave one at each person's seat.

4. **Prepare All Visuals in Advance.** Make sure any electronic presentations or flip charts are set to go. Also, when capturing key points that emerge from group discussion, don't record them verbatim. Use "headlines" to capture on newsprint what participants are saying.

5. **Expedite Subgroup Reporting.** Ask subgroups to list their ideas on flip-chart paper and to post their lists on the walls of the room so that all the work can be viewed and discussed at the same time. Or, going from group to group, have each group report only one item at a time so that everyone can

listen for possible overlap. Subgroups should not repeat what has already been said.

6. **Do Not Allow Discussions to Drag.** Express the need to move on, but be sure in a later discussion to call on those who did not have a chance to contribute previously. Or begin a discussion by first gaining a commitment to a specified time limit and suggesting how many comments can be fit into the allotted time.

7. **Obtain Volunteers Swiftly.** Don't wait for participants to volunteer. You can recruit volunteers during breaks in the session. Continue to call on individual participants if no volunteers speak up immediately. Or use any of the methods in "Ten Alternatives for Assigning Jobs," on page 27.

8. **Be Prepared for Tired or Lethargic Groups.** Provide a list of ideas and questions and ask participants to select ones that are of interest to them; frequently, your list will trigger other thoughts and issues from participants.

9. **Quicken the Pace from Time to Time.** Often, setting time limits for participants energizes them and makes them more productive. Also, use quick-paced techniques such as polling, go-arounds, and partners.

10. **Establish a "Parking Lot."** Agree beforehand that when worthwhile issues arise that are not on the agenda they will be "parked" for later discussion on a separate list.

Ten Props to Employ During Active Meetings

Beyond name tags, tents, overheads, flip charts, refreshments, and other basic supplies, there are a number of props you can utilize to add humor, energy, drama, aesthetics, and focus to a meeting. Here are ten that come to mind.

1. **Hats.** Provide a variety of hats to be worn by participants with designated roles, such as facilitator, recorder, timekeeper, planning committee member, and so forth. Use caps with sports or company logos or buy some inexpensive costume hats.

2. **Posters.** Create posters of familiar quotations that relate to the meeting topics, and display the posters around the room. Not only do they help to create a mood and to generate interest, but you can also use them to begin the meeting by asking participants to choose the quotation that they like the best and to connect the quote to the agenda.

3. **Freebies.** Provide small gifts, such as pens, hand wipes, group photos, toys, or party favors to welcome participants or express appreciation for their coming to the meeting.

4. **Rewards.** Have a supply of stickers, paper money, candy, or any other inexpensive but tangible rewards to acknowledge such things as getting through a difficult decision together, completing a project, finishing on time, or making a special contribution to the group.

5. **Music.** Play recorded music (classical, pop, rock, jazz, reggae, environmental—whatever is relaxing or invigorating) before a meeting or during breaks in the action. (Remember that you may need permission from the music producer. Always check.)

6. **Sound Signals.** You don't need a gavel to call a meeting to order or reconvene a group. There are all kinds of bells and whistles that do the job more pleasantly.

7. **Games.** Simple games and puzzles can be available to occupy people during breaks. Possible choices include Silly Putty®, a yo-yo, a Slinky®, a Koosh® ball, a Nerf® Frisbee™, brain teasers, anagrams, word hunts, or crossword puzzles.

8. **Speaker Identifiers.** Use balls, bean bags, or toy microphones to be passed around to participants who want a turn speaking. Or make a "talking stick" (see p. 169.).

9. **Balloons, Flowers, and Plants.** Use flowers or balloons to decorate the meeting room to create either a party mood, a calm setting, or aesthetic focal points.

10. **Index Cards.** Index cards are one of the most versatile tools to have at any meeting. Use them for inviting written suggestions, for polling, for note taking, for inexpensive name tents, and so on.

Ten Tricks for Calling Participants to Order

When meetings are active, the room can become busy—and even noisy—with small-group activity. From time to time, you will need to call attention to indicate that a time period is up and that you will be leading the group into a new phase. In addition, if there are breaks in a meeting, it helps to have some ways to let participants know that it's time to reconvene. There are several ways to accomplish this, including these.

1. **Use a Sound Signal.** A bell, whistle, or kazoo will do, or use a kitchen timer or other alarm device. Novelty stores also have a variety of sound-making gag toys.

2. **Flick a Light Switch.** This technique isn't offensive if you do it rapidly and keep it brief.

3. **Make a Dramatic Announcement.** Grab attention by saying something like "Testing, 1, 2, 3, testing," "Now hear this, now hear this," or "Earth to group, earth to group." Use a megaphone or microphone for large groups.

4. **Create a Verbal Wave.** Instruct the group to repeat after you whenever they hear you say, "Time's up." In no time at all, the participants will be assisting you in indicating that it is time to stop what they are doing.

5. **Try Clapping.** Instruct the group members to clap their hands once if they can hear your instructions. Within a few

seconds, the first participants to hear your instructions will clap; by doing so, they will get the rest of the group's attention.

6. **Play Prerecorded Music.** Select music that can quickly command attention. You may elect to call participants back gently, using meditative music, or with a bang, using something like the opening bar of Beethoven's Fifth.

7. **Use a Silent Signal.** Explain to participants that they should quiet down whenever they see you using a particular signal (for example, holding up your index and middle fingers). Encourage the participants to use the signal when you do.

8. **Tell a Joke.** Inform participants that you have a storehouse of jokes or riddles that will serve as a cue to bring a meeting back to order.

9. **"Can We Talk?"** Use Joan Rivers' famous line as a way to reconvene the entire group for discussion.

10. **Announce "Break Time!"** This will surely capture everyone's attention.

Ten Methods to Deal with Difficult Participants

Just using active meeting techniques tends to minimize the problems some difficult participants create. Nonetheless, difficulties such as monopolizing, distracting, and withdrawing still may occur. Below are ten interventions you can use; some work well with individual participants, while others work with the entire group.

1. **Signal Nonverbally.** Make eye contact with or move closer to participants who hold private conversations, start to fall asleep, or hide from participation. Press your fingers together to signal for a wordy participant to finish what he or she is saying. Make a "T" sign with your fingers to stop unwanted behavior.

2. **Listen Actively.** When participants monopolize discussion, go off on a tangent, or argue with you, interject with a summary of their views and then ask others to speak. Or acknowledge the value of the person's viewpoints and invite him or her to discuss them with you during a break.

3. **Encourage New Volunteers.** When a few participants repeatedly speak up in meetings while others hold back, pose a question or issue and then ask how many people have a response to it. You should see new hands go up. Call on someone who hasn't spoken previously.

4. **Invoke Participation Rules.** From time to time, tell participants that you would like to use rules such as the following:

   - Only participants who have not yet spoken can participate.

   - Each new comment must build on a previous idea.

   - Speak for yourself, not for others.

5. **Use Good-Natured Humor.** One way to deflect difficult behavior is to use humor. Be careful, however, not to be sarcastic or patronizing. Gently rib the participant about inappropriate behavior ("You certainly have a lot to say!") or humorously put yourself down instead of the participant ("I guess I lost my concentration for awhile.").

6. **Connect on a Personal Level.** Even if a problem participant is hostile or withdrawn, make a point of getting to know the person during a break in the meeting. It is unlikely that people will continue to give you a hard time or remain distant if you have taken an interest in them.

7. **Change the Method of Participation.** Sometimes, you can control the damage done by difficult participants by inserting new formats, such as using pairs or small groups rather than full-group discussion.

8. **Ignore Mildly Negative Behavior.** Try to pay little or no attention to behavior that is a small nuisance. These types of behavior may disappear if you simply continue the meeting.

9. **Discuss Very Negative Behavior Privately.** You must call a stop to behavior that you find detrimental to the meeting. Arrange a break and firmly request, in private, a change in behavior of those participants who are disruptive. Or create small-group activities and call aside the problem participants. If the entire group is involved, stop the meeting and explain clearly what you need from participants to conduct the meeting effectively.

10. **Don't Take It Personally.** Remember that many problem behaviors have nothing to do with you. Instead, they are due to personal fears and needs or displaced anger. Try to determine whether this is the case, and ask whether participants can put aside whatever is affecting their positive involvement in the meeting.

Ten Energizers to Wake Up or Relax a Group

There are many simple, short activities you can use to energize a tired group or to help a tense group calm down. You can do any of the following at the beginning of a meeting, after a break, or right in the middle of the action.

1. **Singing a Round.** Section off participants and invite them to sing a familiar round such as *Row, Row, Row Your Boat.*

2. **Slow Breathing.** Invite participants to take ten slow, cleansing breaths . . . inhaling deeply and then exhaling. Then, invite them to reverse the process . . . slowly exhaling and then inhaling. Even though breathing is always a continuous cycle of inhaling and exhaling, consciously trying to emphasize each part of the cycle can be quite exhilarating.

3. **Yawning Contest.** See who can yawn the loudest or the longest.

4. **Touch Blue.** Call out a color (such as blue), and have participants scurry to touch any object of that color or the person wearing it. Identify other dimensions besides colors, such as "something glass" or " something round," or mention specific objects, such as a watch, a book, sneakers, and so forth. Call the next item as soon as everyone has touched the current one.

5. **Do the Hokey, Pokey.** You know: "Put your right (foot, arm, hip, etc.) in, put your right (foot, arm, hip, etc.) out, put your

right (foot, arm, hip, etc.) in, and shake it all about. Do the hokey, pokey, and turn yourself around. That's what it's all about."

6. **Titles.** Give participants one minute to shout out the titles of as many films or books as they can. To make it more challenging, create more specifics, such as Hitchcock films, books by John Grisham, war films, management books, and so forth.

7. **Paper Airplanes.** Give out sheets of paper and challenge participants to make a paper airplane that goes the farthest or successfully hits a bull's-eye you have drawn on a flip chart.

8. **Mirroring.** Pair up participants and have one of the pair (call that person the "leader") do hand or stretching motions while the other person (call that person the "follower") simultaneously imitates or "mirrors" the partner's motions. Invite participants to switch roles, and even to switch partners.

9. **Back Rubs.** Pair up participants and invite them to give each other back rubs. Or have participants line up in a circle, turning in the same direction. Have them give a back rub to the person in front of them. Then, have them turn in the opposite direction and give a back rub to the person in front of them.

10. **Human Knot.** Ask participants to form a circle and clasp hands with two other people opposite them. Then, ask them to unravel the tangle of hands and arms that has been created, but without releasing their hands. The activity ends when the original circle is intact.

Ten Things to Do When the Group Is Stuck

....

At times, a group seems to be spinning its wheels at a meeting. The participants may be tired, distracted, unfocused, apathetic, uncreative, or indecisive. You might try any of the ideas below to help the group free itself and start the wheels turning again.

1. **Take a Break.** Sometimes, this simple step will revitalize a group.

2. **Change Seats.** Ask participants to change their seats. This may give people a new vantage point.

3. **Break into Pairs.** This can be a good change of pace from whole-group discussion and should loosen everyone's thinking.

4. **Write Down Ideas.** Have the participants stop talking and start writing down their thoughts. Consider inviting them to write with their non-dominant hand. This practice is known to open up the brain. Or invite group members to draw an idea rather than put it in words.

5. **Turn Out or Dim the Lighting.** It's zany, but it may focus distracted participants.

6. **Have a Stand-Up Discussion.** Simply ask participants to continue the meeting for a few minutes while standing. Mention that "we often think better on our feet."

7. **Poll Participants.** Take a quick survey of opinions or a straw (nonbinding) poll about decision options, or take a quick pulse of the mood of the group.

8. **Create a Time Deadline.** Often, when you say, "Okay, let's just give this another 5 minutes," you accelerate participation.

9. **Move On to Something Else.** Putting a matter on hold and returning to it later can be a useful way of dealing with an issue.

10. **Assign or Defer to a Subgroup.** Consider the option of letting a smaller number of people tackle the issue.

Ten Tips to Make Flip Charts Graphic

The value of recording ideas or information on a flip chart is well-established. Participants are more focused and team-oriented. There are many things you can do to enliven flip charts.

1. **Use of Color.** Use black, blue, green, or purple for text. Alternate these colors to create contrast. Highlight with red, orange, or pink to add flair.

2. **Sticky Notes.** Apply self-sticking notes, stars, and dots to flip-chart paper as a way to list, rearrange, vote, or highlight.

3. **Lettering.** Use uppercase letters for TITLES or HEADLINES and when you wish to EMPHASIZE key words. Combine Upper and Lower Case Letters for Text. Draw attention with **SHADOW** lettering, add thickness or details to the letters, or try Hollow lettering.

4. **Numbers and Bullets.** Number items when it makes it easier if you can refer to them by number. Otherwise, provide bullets, such as dots, stars, check marks, or other symbols.

5. **Symbols.** Use other graphically appealing symbols, such as arrows, circles, and boxes to separate words and phrases. Apply different styles to these symbols to build them up or make them hollow.

6. **Word Pictures.** Use a visual image to convey words, such as a *light bulb* to convey "idea," a set of *steps* to convey a "series of actions," a *cloud* to convey "unclear," and a *thumbs up* to convey "agreement."

7. **Mind Mapping.** Rather than using a conventional, linear list, place a key word (for example, "cost cutting") in the center of the paper and surround it with elaborating ideas.

8. **White Space.** Less is more. Provide wide margins for text, use very few words or symbols, or place things in unusual places (on the bottom, on the side, off-center, and so forth).

9. **Clustering.** Emphasize ideas in common by underlining them or circling them in the same color.

10. **Cartooning.** Draw a face with a circle filled in with simple dots and lines to convey facial expressions. Draw a full body by using stick figures or balloons.

Ten Questions to Process a Meeting

Before meetings end, hold a brief discussion in which participants reflect on how they worked as a group *(teamwork)* and on what was accomplished *(productivity)*. Here is an array of final questions to use to start this processing.

1. How well did the meeting match your expectations?
2. What are you taking away from this meeting? What is the group taking away?
3. How did we work together? What was helpful? Not helpful?
4. How could we have been more efficient today? More effective? More inclusive?
5. If we were to have this meeting all over again, what, in hindsight, should we do the next time?
6. What was the best part of our meeting? The worst?
7. Are you hopeful or are you concerned about the progress we are making?
8. What should we do differently next time? What should we continue doing?
9. What suggestions do you have for our next meeting?
10. How many of you would volunteer to help plan our next meeting?

Preparing Active Meetings

You have a meeting scheduled. If you're like most meeting leaders, you hope the meeting will go well. People will show up. They will be well-prepared and eager to participate. They will observe good meeting etiquette. A lot will be accomplished.

You might be lucky and all these things will happen. However, a meeting leader or facilitator who doesn't want to leave things up to chance must work actively and well in advance of the meeting to ensure its success.

This section of *101 Ways to Make Meetings Active* covers twelve strategies to help you prepare participants for an active meeting. They are arranged in order by when you would undertake them. The earlier strategies might require work on your part or the part of others from one week to one month before the scheduled meeting. The later strategies will involve you and/or others closer to the day of the meeting.

Because these strategies are not used during the actual meeting, they will not be coded in terms of group size, time required, and fun quotient. They are intended for any meeting situation.

Building an Active Agenda in Advance

Overview

The preparation of an agenda is the first step in planning any meeting. An "active" agenda communicates to participants how to prepare for and participate in an upcoming meeting. Here is a process to create a meeting agenda that encourages involvement and participation.

Procedure

1. By yourself or with an agenda planning committee, develop an overall POP.

   - *Purpose:* For what purpose(s) is the meeting being held?
   - *Outcome:* What do you want the results of the meeting to be?
   - *Plan:* What needs to happen at the meeting for it to meet its purpose and achieve the expected results?

   Also consider asking potential participants for their POP suggestions.

2. Proceed to more detailed planning by identifying agenda

items that will achieve the overall POP. Classify the purpose of agenda items into the following categories:

- For your information
- For initial discussion and feedback
- For developing action ideas
- For a decision
- For detailed planning and implementation

3. Prepare a simple written agenda by listing:

- Date, time, and location of the meeting
- Names and contact information for invited participants
- Agenda items planned for the meeting
- Tentative time allotted to each item on the agenda
- Person(s) responsible for each agenda item
- Purpose of each item

A sample agenda is given on the following page.

4. For each agenda item, create a *participation guide,* which should include:

- Background and any update (provide some background information and any new information)
- Reference material, including any information participants should bring with them
- Preparation requests, such as pre-reading, information gathering, proposal writing, or anything you want participants to do to prepare for this meeting
- Discussion questions (indicate key questions to be discussed for each agenda item)

Attach the participation guide to the agenda.

District C Administrator's Conference Agenda

Date: September 17

Time: 1:00–4:00

Location: 101 Spring St., Room 202

Participants: Joe (joe@SVS.edu), Andy (andy@SVS.edu),
Chris(chris@SVS.edu), Helen (helen@SVS.edu),
Pat (pat@SVS.edu), Derrick(derrick@SVS.edu),
Ruth (ruth@SVS.edu), Taka (taka@SVS.edu)

Topic	Purpose	Time	Person Responsible
Personal Updates	icebreaker	10	Helen
State Funding	initial discussion	40	Andy
District Lunch Program	decision	45	Chris
New Hiring Standards	information	10	Ruth
Energy Consumption	planning	60	Joe
Processing of Meeting	evaluation	15	Pat

---

5. Request comments and questions about the agenda in advance. Even if there are none, you have signaled your intention to have an active meeting when it does take place.

Variation

Communicate any special processes you will use in the meeting, such as the ones recommended later in this book.

2

Pre-Meeting Survey of Participants

Overview

A survey can be used before a single meeting or a series of meetings to assess the participants. Often, the data that is collected can be fed back to the participants in summary form in advance of or at the beginning of a meeting. This way, everyone knows what information was obtained. The information may also be helpful in planning or finalizing the agenda and meeting plan.

Procedure

1. Determine what information would be useful to obtain from participants. Consider some of the following categories:

   - Participant demographics ("How many years have you worked here?")

   - Job descriptions ("What are your supervisory duties?")

   - Prior experience ("Have you served on a selection committee before?")

   - Expectations about the meeting ("Do you think we will finish our final report?")

- Attitudes toward this meeting ("Are you optimistic about the outcome of this meeting?")
- Opinions about a meeting issue ("Do you think our conversion plan will work?")
- Resources available ("Are you on-line?")
- Agenda suggestions ("What would you like to add to the agenda?")

2. Develop the actual survey. Use a variety of survey techniques that make the completion of the survey quick and easy and allow for some tabulation of results, such as:

- Rating scales

I think the conversion plan is effective.
strongly agree   agree   not sure   disagree   strongly disagree

---

- Ranking or prioritizing items

Rank the importance of each agenda item to you, with "1" as the highest priority.
_____budget projections
_____fund raising ideas
_____personnel review
_____building community

- Checklist

How do you feel about our upcoming meeting?
   (Circle all the words or phrases that apply.)

hopeful   pessimistic   too ambitious   excited   too long

overdue   not needed   confused   on target   not prepared

- Sentence stem

> **Complete this sentence:**
> **One thing that concerns me about the meeting is. . . .**

- Short answer

> **Describe your prior experience with fund raising:**

3. Show the survey to a colleague and obtain feedback from him or her about its content, clarity, and user-friendliness. Make any modifications desired.

4. Send the survey to participants. Explain its purpose and be specific about the benefits everyone will obtain if it is completed and returned on time. Be sure to specify a deadline. A sample cover letter is on the following page.

Dear Participant,

I will be serving as the facilitator for our all-day long-range planning commission meeting.

Our organization is making a clear commitment to its own continued growth and development, and I hope that you will see this day as a valuable opportunity to communicate with other participants about our visions for the future—without the constraints of daily deadlines.

As a guide to planning this meeting, I am gathering ideas and opinions from everyone in order to share them with the group for discussion at our meeting. Please join with your colleagues in filling out the attached survey. Your honest responses will enable all of us to have a clear picture of the group.

Your responses will be totally anonymous. I will summarize the results and report back to everyone at the first meeting.

Thank you in advance for your cooperation and support. I look forward to working with you.

Variation

If the group is small, interview each participant individually.

3

Advance Reviews

Overview

When a meeting is especially important and the number of participants is large, it may be beneficial to bring together a small group to obtain members' feedback on the agenda and/or the design of the meeting. Or you could even try portions of the meeting agenda as a "dry run." Here is a process you can utilize.

Procedure

1. Decide whether you want to obtain input and feedback about the meeting plan from a small group or conduct a dry run of the meeting.

2. For the former, ask people you select to participate in an "advisory planning group" session. Explain that you would like to obtain (choose one or more of the following):

   • Reactions to the meeting agenda you have already set

   • Suggestions for a meeting agenda not yet set

   • Views about issues pertaining to the meeting agenda

3. For the latter, invite a small group of people to participate in a "dry run" of the meeting so that you can obtain preliminary indications of the effectiveness of your meeting plan. Think of it as a dress rehearsal. You may decide to cover the entire meeting or only a part of it. You can also walk through parts of the meeting plan with participants, rather than have them actually experience them. Be sure to ask participants to review your meeting plan.

4. Whichever way you choose to obtain reviews in advance, select people to invite on any of the following bases:

   - Random selection
   - A representative sample of the entire group
   - Influential participants

Preparation Is Everyone's Responsibility

Overview

When participants are well-prepared, the meeting is more likely to prove successful. Part of meeting planning involves determining what you want participants to do prior to the meeting. Here are some suggestions.

Procedure

1. Determine what you would like participants to do in order to be well-prepared and to make the meeting a productive and interesting one. Here are some activities to consider. Use one or all of them, or combine a few to meet your needs.

   • Assign background reading, either to the group as a whole or parceled out by topic to different subgroups or individuals.

     For example, ask a staff of nurses to read new hospital regulations prior to the meeting.

   • If you offer the same assignment to the entire group, ask each person to report on a different aspect of the assignment.

For example, ask each person on a future planning group to read a different proposal.

- Ask participants to interview others to collect information to be discussed at the meeting.

  For example, a member of a public school board, looking forward to voting on a certain program, may want to obtain first-hand information by asking questions of administrators, faculty members, and students.

- Assign different people to seek information from different sources and then have the participants compare notes.

  For example, if the topic is to decide how to renovate a building, have members investigate items such as costs, building contractors, and level of satisfaction that other organizations have experienced when doing similar projects.

- Ask an individual participant or a small group to conduct a simple research project or experiment.

  For example, a participant might be asked to conduct a time and motion study.

- Ask one of the more knowledgeable members of the group to prepare a proposal required by your business or organization.

  For example, a businessperson might be asked to develop a business plan for a charity organization to which he or she belongs.

2. Communicate your wish that participants come to the meeting prepared. Be specific about the assignment you'd like them to complete and by when.

3. It's a good idea to ask the participants to forward any useful information to you prior to the meeting, if possible, so you can create a workable agenda. E-mail is perfect for this kind

of communication; however, if group members don't have access to e-mail, encourage them to telephone you or mail their data to you as early as possible.

Variations

1. If new information could help the group to make a decision at the meeting, ask participants to search for fresh data on the Internet or even on their organization's intranet.

2. Do not overlook the old reliable sources, such as newspapers or magazines, for new ideas. This type of research can be assigned to a person who does not have access to a computer.

5

Stating Expectations Up-Front

Overview

Stating expectations up-front for those who will be taking part in a meeting is a good idea. Giving participants advance notice of what is expected of them allows them time to plan how they will contribute to the group.

Procedure

1. The expectations should be prepared in writing and sent by mail or e-mail.

2. You might want to consider the following categories as you establish expectations for a particular series of meetings:

   - **Attendance.** Make it clear that participants are expected to attend all meetings. Discuss what might be considered a legitimate excuse for missing a meeting, and together establish a method for participants to notify you or another designated leader if they find it impossible to attend.

   - **Promptness.** Promise that meetings will start and end on time. Make clear to the participants what "on time" means to you and what it will mean to them if they are to take part in a productive effort.

- **Meeting Time and Place.** Establish a regular meeting time and place, if you can, and indicate to participants how and when you will either notify them or remind them of meetings.

- **Participation.** Emphasize that each participant is a valuable member of the group and impress on each that he or she should both listen attentively and also speak freely. Tell them that constructive dissent is welcome, but that they should observe normal conversational courtesies.

- **Responsibility.** Outline any responsibilities you will assume, as well as those you expect participants to adopt during the meeting.

- **Interruptions**. Be specific about any limits you want to place on accepting incoming telephone calls, returning calls from beepers and pagers, leaving the meeting room, and other possible interruptions. Identify how messages will be delivered during the meeting (for example, by message board or through a contact telephone number during the meeting).

- **Follow-Up.** Inform participants what they will be asked to do after the meeting.

6

Be Our Guest

Overview

As any job applicant knows, first appearances are important. Why should it be any different with meeting announcements? The tone of the standard meeting announcement, which tends to be formal and dry, may carry over into the meeting itself. Why not find a more exciting way to announce the meeting? Send participants invitations that will grab their attention. Chances are that more people will attend the meeting, and they'll arrive with better attitudes.

Procedure

1. Prepare the invitations early, making sure to allow adequate time for mail delivery. Include all pertinent information, such as date, time, and place, a brief line or two about the purpose of the meeting, and a quick outline of the agenda.

2. An easy way to dress up a meeting notice or invitation is to add a little color. Either use colored paper or make a border on the sheet. You could even outline a company logo on white paper with a colorful felt-tipped marker.

3. Consider carefully the tone you want to set for the meeting. If you're planning for a charity event, such as a concert, why not sprinkle some shiny confetti musical notes into the envelope or paste them on both invitation and envelope? Or decorate the sheet with a cartoon of the composer or artist. If the group is planning to build a new hospital, buy or make little cutouts of construction equipment and decorate both invitation and envelope with those. How about bright green dollar signs on an invitation to the finance committee? Using a little imagination will pay off handsomely in an active meeting.

4. An important part of the invitation is the RSVP. Always include an RSVP card and allow choices such as:

   - *I will be there.*
   - *I will be willing to help in planning the meeting.*
   - *I can't come, but will find someone to replace me.*
   - *I can't come, but please let me know what happens.*
   - *I have some thoughts about some of the agenda items. Please contact me.*
   - *I will bring (refreshments, equipment, records, resource material).*

   Be sure to ask them to indicate the specific refreshments or equipment being brought.

Here's an example of a meeting invitation:

Be Our Guest

YOU ARE INVITED TO A MEETING OF THE
JEFFERSON DAY SCHOOL BOARD OF DIRECTORS.
DATE: AUGUST 15
TIME: 7 TO 10 P.M.
PLACE: 374 JEFFERSON STREET, MAIN CONFERENCE ROOM

BACKGROUND: Jefferson Hospital administrators have asked the day school to consider expanding its program and facilities to accommodate children of hospital workers.

SITUATION: The hospital has vacant land on the south side of Jefferson Street across from our facility and would consider constructing a building large enough to house those currently enrolled in the day school, as well as children of hospital employees. Although there are obvious advantages to this idea, we also need to discuss any drawbacks before we meet with the hospital board.

RSVP by August 7 to   Robin Keller
Jefferson Day School
374 Jefferson St.
Chicago, IL 60637
or fax to 312-791-8420

_____*I WILL ATTEND.*
_____*I WILL TALK TO SOME DAY SCHOOL PARENTS TO*
SOLICIT THEIR IDEAS.
_____*I WILL BRING RESOURCE MATERIAL.*
_____*I WILL BRING REFRESHMENTS.*
_____*I CANNOT ATTEND, BUT LET ME KNOW WHAT HAPPENS.*

_____

                                                    NAME

7

Creative Name Tents

Overview

Name tents serve as meeting place cards. They are a good way to identify participants without using formal introductions. Participants feel welcome when they find their names at specific places. Name tents also help to avoid quibbling over seating. Here are some ways to be creative with them.

Procedure

1. Either make name tents yourself or buy them. All you have to do is use sheets of paper sufficiently heavy to stand alone, fold them in half, print participants' names on them, and place on the tables at each seat. (If you facilitate meetings for large groups often, you might want to consider purchasing reusable, write-on/wipe-off name tents.)

2. When you provide name tents, you also have an opportunity to have a little fun, to lighten the mood of the meeting, and to make people feel more comfortable.

3. These are some ideas to keep in mind:

- Be sure to write names on both front and back of the tents.

- Remember that extra space on the tents is a good place for messages or slogans. Look at them the way a marketing person looks at advertising space.

- You may want to color-code the tents in some way to identify subgroups. The tents themselves may be made of colored paper.

- Use a felt-tipped marker to design a colorful border on the tent or merely stick on the kind of colored dots available at any stationery or office supply store.

- On the back of the tent, add a "participation suggestion," such as "Learn to listen, listen to learn" or "Keep an open mind."

- If you have enough space, list the key points of the meeting's agenda to remind participants what has to be accomplished.

- Try writing a simple riddle or brain teaser on the tent, but not one so complicated that it will distract the participant.

- A short joke written on the tent will bring a smile to the participant and others seated nearby.

- Short quotes often offer food for thought and help inspire action. Find them in a dictionary of quotations.

8

Exciting Meeting Packets

Overview

Receiving individual packets filled with meeting information offers people the same elation they feel when they go to a dinner party and find the table already set. It signifies that the host is ready and waiting after a careful preparation for the guests' arrival. The presence of a packet shows that you have thoughtfully provided information you believe will be useful for them. A packet of information is particularly important for larger meetings. It will save you a lot of distribution time and commotion.

Procedure

1. Select as fine a folder as your organization can afford, preferably one with your organization's logo.

2. In each folder, always place items such as:

   - A pencil or an inexpensive ball-point pen.
   - A copy of the agenda for the meeting.
   - A list of participants and information about how to contact them. (Include a seating plan, if one is used for the meeting.)

- Reference materials related to the task or project at hand, such as newspaper or magazine articles about similar projects, copies of budgets, cost estimates, letters, or statements to be read and discussed.

- Enough paper for detailed notes. If the topics you are addressing are complex, create a special note-taking format, setting aside specific areas on the pages for a brief description of each topic, main points of discussion, decisions or outcomes and, if applicable, what is to happen next.

- A few index cards, perhaps in different colors for various purposes. They can be useful in a variety of ways; for example, if you need a quick survey of the participants, simply ask them to write "yes," "no," or "maybe" on a card and hold it up. The cards may also be used to solicit ideas or opinions about the topics of the meeting itself. They can be collected as the participants leave.

3. An optional idea is to provide a list of positive meeting behaviors to remind people that they are expected to be considerate, open, participatory, and so forth. Add a friendly note asking them to turn off their cell phones and pagers. In the unlikely event of a real emergency, ask that they leave the meeting room to make a call in order to minimize disruption and distraction for others.

4. Include a sheet listing directions for stress-reduction or energy-boosting activities, either mental or physical.

5. If the meeting is to be an especially long one, provide a picture of the pink Energizer® bunny as a whimsical touch. You might want also to include a stick of sugar-free gum or a couple of mints, a Chinese fortune cookie, or even small candies as a refreshing surprise.

6. It's especially important to provide housekeeping information if the meeting involves large numbers and is taking

place in a building unfamiliar to many participants. A layout of the building should show the location of the following:

- Meeting rooms
- Rest rooms
- Telephones
- Computer areas
- Refreshment areas
- Stairways, escalators, and elevators
- Emergency exits
- Safe parking facilities
- Special facilities for the disabled.

9

Facilitator Prompt Cards

Overview

A good meeting should be conducted like an intelligent conversation—with active participation from all parties. Like a sailboat, the meeting can be blown off course. Prompt cards are an unusual, but effective, way to control the progress of the meeting without interfering with the action. They can even supply a little comic relief to ease tense moments.

Procedure

1. Prepare the prompt cards before the meeting. Some examples of phrases for the cards are listed here:

Good Idea	*Watch the Time*
Let's Move On	*Agree to Disagree?*
Decision Time?	*More Ideas?*
Time for a Break	*New Participants, Please*

   The cards should be big enough, with lettering bold enough, that participants cannot mistake their message. The proper size for the cards will depend on the number of participants. You must make sure that even a person in the back row can see them.

2. Use index stock, and consider adding graphics. The graphic material should be simple and convey the message instantaneously.

3. Use the cards to prompt the group without verbally interrupting anyone. Display the cards to the participants at the beginning of the meeting and explain that you will be holding one up silently when you believe the occasion warrants its use to help the meeting along.

Variations

1. You may want to spread the cards on a table or hang them on a nearby wall and let participants use them when they believe they would be useful.

2. Prepare an occasional extra-large card for emphasis. For example, instead of using a standard 4" x 6" card bearing the words, "Great idea," display a huge sheet of 11" x 17" paper marked "GREAT IDEA" for an exceptional idea. The message will be unmistakable, and it will help to flag the idea's significance for the group.

3. A particularly relevant cartoon may also be effective. For example, if the group has reached an impasse over an idea, a cartoon of an old car stuck in the mud may bring a smile to the participants and show them exactly where they stand.

4. If you're working with a technical group, you might want to include some meaningful technical terms on the cards. This will help to put the participants at ease and should also increase rapport.

10

Going Beyond Minutes

Overview

Keeping up-to-date written records may be one of the most neglected, as well as one of the most important, aspects of the meeting process. When complex issues are addressed, it's especially important to maintain a complete file of activities and assignments.

Procedure

1. Before the meeting, make sure the person assigned to take minutes is aware of the importance you place on accurate and complete information.

2. Request that this person include:
   - The date and time of the meeting
   - Names of those attending
   - Topics discussed
   - Points made during discussions
   - Actions taken or decisions made

- Tasks to be performed
- Items to be carried over to the next agenda

Here's an example of a simple form for minutes that you can adapt to your particular group:

Name of Group_____   **Name of Minute Taker**_____

Date, time, and place of meeting   _____

List of members attending:

_____   _____

_____   _____

_____   _____

_____   _____

_____   _____

_____   _____

Summarize topics and decisions:

Items placed in "future" file:

Date selected for next meeting: _____

Ask that the minutes be sent to all participants as quickly as possible after the meeting.

3. You may also want to ask another person attending the meeting to keep a "follow-up" list, showing who has volunteered to take on certain tasks and also noting the date when he or she will complete that task.

4. Assign someone to be a group record keeper. Records go beyond minutes and include such items as documents, lists from brainstorming sessions, charts, tapes, and proposals. Records serve as quick references in case a report needs to be drawn up for another company, the community, or for another organization you want to join your campaign. Good records, especially those concerned with long-term projects, can be used by new members to catch up, and they can be used to keep current members informed.

Preparing the Meeting Space

Overview

It is absolutely necessary to be sure everything in the meeting space is ready for participants. Make a thorough check of the room before the meeting to be sure it's clean, well-lighted, and at the right temperature before people arrive. This is one place where appearance definitely does matter. People will be more at ease, and more able to concentrate, if the room is comfortable and clean.

Procedure

1. Devise a checklist to follow in preparing the meeting space. Consider each of these items:

   • **Lighting.** Make sure the room is appropriately lighted, especially if the meeting is held in the evening. People will be more open to talking to one another in a well-lighted area. In addition, you don't want participants to have to strain to see when there is paperwork to be done.

   • **Cleanliness.** Check that the room has been properly cleaned and that there is no residue on the tables, that whiteboards are clean, that ash trays are available and clean (unless it is a nonsmoking facility), and that the trash has been emptied.

- **Audiovisuals.** Set up any audiovisual equipment and make sure that it operates properly. Do a test run.

- **Flip Charts.** Evaluate whether there are enough easels, newsprint sheets, rolls of masking tape, and workable marking pens. Hang any prepared lists on the walls, as well as any graphics or other charts. Be sure to hang an "unfinished business" or "parking lot" sheet on the wall where items for future meetings or creative ideas that may threaten to get the meeting off track may be stored for later consideration.

- **Temperature.** The right temperature for a meeting room is pleasantly cool. Keep in mind that as the room fills up, the temperature will rise a little. It's probably better to have the room a bit too cool than too hot. That's at least intellectually stimulating, and people will feel more energized.

- **Air Quality.** If the air is stale, open the windows immediately or turn on the air conditioner or a fan to clear out the air. Do the same if there's even a lingering hint of smoke. Although some facilitators like to use an air freshener before a meeting, if you choose that option, do it with a light hand. The "freshness" of some commercial products can be truly daunting. A small bowl of potpourri offers a sweeter solution.

- **Nearby Noise.** Select a room as far removed from outside noise as you possibly can. If you have to use a room in a building near a busy street, don't forget how noisy traffic can be. Also, check to be sure that no one will be using noisy machines nearby.

- **Music.** You might want to play some light background music, especially if your group breaks into smaller groups for discussion, as the music helps to block out other conversations.

- **Furniture.** Make sure there are enough tables and chairs for your needs. If not, find more. Check for broken furniture and replace it as soon as possible.

- **Size and Layout.** Almost last, but not least, try to match the size of the room to the number of people expected. If that's not an option, and you find the meeting space too large for the group, adjust tables and chairs to set the occupied area of the room off in some way. Arrange furniture using the suggestions from "Ten Layouts for Setting Up a Meeting Room" on page 3.

Active Participation in Videoconference Meetings*

Overview

Because of the increasing availability of videoconferencing technology, more and more meetings are held with participants who are geographically dispersed. Active participation in videoconference meetings can be challenging because the meeting experience is usually more stilted, and the communication flow can be frustrating. Here are some ways to overcome the obstacles.

Procedure

1. Decide carefully who should be attending the meeting at each site. Minimizing the number of participants maximizes the visibility of each participant, the conversation flow, and the overall human connection.

2. To create more intimacy when participants are strangers to one another, ask participants to send photos, biographies, and personal tidbits about themselves to others prior to the first meeting.

_____

*Based on strategies developed by Jana Markowitz.

3. Videoconference meetings should be especially well-planned. Provide meeting materials far in advance and suggest ways for participants to be well-prepared.

4. Prepare in advance visual material that can be viewed clearly by all parties during the meeting. The less you rely on an auditory exchange of information (as opposed to discussion) the better.

5. Establish "participation" signals. Participants can be asked to do any of the following to gain permission to speak:

   • Raise their hands

   • Say the facilitator's name first ("Chris, I have an idea on this.")

   • Say their own names first ("Pat James here. I have an idea.")

   • Tap the table in front of them

   • Whistle

   • Use some kind of a sound signal

6. To equalize participation, take turns deliberately, going from meeting site to meeting site. Say, for example, "Let's hear from the Atlanta group for the next 5 minutes." Or you might rotate among sites for one brief contribution each.

7. Follow up each meeting with exchanges through ordinary e-mail or through discussion databases such as Lotus Notes®. You could also use an electronic meeting system that allows for same-time (synchronous) discussion without having to use videoconferencing facilities.

Engaging Participants from the Start

When you're starting a meeting, it's important to resist the temptation to get right down to business. Instead, you must do some things quickly to establish a climate for teamwork. These preliminaries to the actual "meat" of the agenda are intended to do the following:

- Help participants become acquainted or reacquainted
- Build team cohesion and collaborative attitudes
- Focus participants away from outside distractions and toward the business at hand
- Explain how the meetings will be organized and managed

In a single meeting, you might choose only one of the sixteen engagement strategies in this section. However, if you are beginning a multiple-session team or group meeting, the investment of time conducting several of these activities will be rewarded many times over. If you leave the group dynamics to chance, chances are there will be many individual agendas and uneven participation.

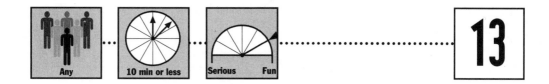

Human Scavenger Hunt

Overview

This is a popular icebreaker that can be designed in a number of ways and for any number of people. It helps to introduce people and uses physical movement right up-front to energize a meeting.

Procedure

1. Prepare six to ten descriptive statements to complete the phrase "Find someone who. . . ." Include statements that identify personal information and/or meeting topics. Use some of these beginnings:

   Find someone who . . .
   - likes/enjoys _____
   - knows what a _____
   - thinks that _____
   - specializes _____
   - has already _____
   - is motivated by _____
   - believes that _____

- has recently read a book about_____
- dislikes_____
- has a great idea for_____
- owns_____
- wants_____

2. Hand out the statements and give the following instructions: *"This is like a scavenger hunt, except that you are looking for people instead of objects. When I say 'begin,' go around the room looking for people who match the statements I handed out. You can use each person for only one statement, even if he or she matches more than one. When you have found a match, write down the person's first name on the appropriate blank."*

3. When most people have finished, stop the hunt and gather together the full group.

4. You may want to offer a token prize to the person who finishes first. More importantly, survey the full group about each of the items. Promote short discussions of some of the items that might be brought up at the meeting.

Variations

1. Avoid competition entirely by allowing enough time for everyone to complete the hunt.

2. Ask participants to meet others and find out how many matches can be made with each person.

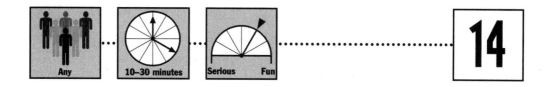

Any   **10–30 minutes**   **Serious   Fun**   **14**

Group Résumé

Overview

Putting together a group résumé is a fun-filled way to help people become acquainted. Or it can even be used for some team building at a meeting at which members already know one another. The activity can even accomplish part of your work for you if you gear it to the topic of the meeting.

Procedure

1. To do a group résumé, divide the meeting participants into subgroups of three to six members each.

2. Tell the participants that they represent an incredible array of talents and experiences!

3. Suggest that one way to identify and brag about the group's resources is to compose a group résumé.

4. Give the subgroups newsprint and markers to use in creating their résumés, which should include any information that promotes the *subgroup as a whole*. (You may want to help them get started by suggesting a job or contract the organization could be bidding for.) The groups may choose to

include any of the following information:

- Educational background
- Knowledge about the meeting subject
- Total years of professional experience
- Positions held
- Professional skills
- Major accomplishments
- Publications
- Hobbies, talents, travel, family

5. Invite each subgroup to present its résumé and celebrate the total resources of the members.

Variations

1. To speed up the activity, hand out a prepared résumé outline that indicates information that needs to be compiled.

2. Instead of having participants compile a résumé, ask them to interview one another about categories that you provide.

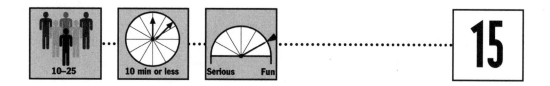

The Company You Keep

Overview

This activity introduces physical movement right from the start of your meeting and helps participants to become acquainted. It moves rapidly and is a lot of fun.

Procedure

1. Make a list of categories you think might be appropriate in a getting-acquainted activity for the meeting you're planning. Sample categories include the following:

   - Month of birth

   - Negative or positive reaction to (identify a topic, such as poetry, role playing, science, or computers)

   - Number of hours of sleep nightly

   - Favorite (identify any item, such as a color, sport, or fast-food restaurant)

   - Left-handed or right-handed writer

   - Shoe color

   - Agreement or disagreement with any statement of opinion

on an issue, for example, "Affirmative action has not been effective."

2. Clear some floor space so that participants can move around freely.

3. Call out a category. Direct participants to locate as quickly as possible all the people whom, given the category, they would "associate with." For example, "right-handers" and "left-handers" would separate into two groups. Or those who agree with a statement would separate from those who disagree. If the category contains more than two choices (for example, the month of birth), ask participants to congregate with those like them, thereby forming several groups.

4. After participants form the appropriate clusters, ask them to shake hands with "the company you keep." Invite all the participants to observe approximately how many people there are in different groups.

5. Go immediately to the next category. Keep the participants moving from group to group as you announce new categories.

6. Gather the entire group together. Discuss the diversity of participants revealed by the activity.

Variations

1. Ask participants to locate people who are different from them rather than the same. For example, you might ask participants to find people who have eyes of a different color from theirs.

2. Invite participants to suggest categories.

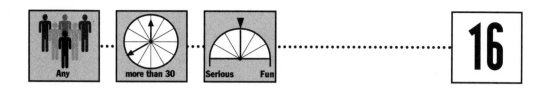

Getting to Know You Well

Overview

Most getting-acquainted activities are limited opportunities to meet others. An alternative is to arrange an in-depth experience in which pairs of participants can become really well acquainted.

Procedure

1. Form the participants into pairs in any manner you desire. Criteria for forming pairs might include any of the following:

   - Two participants who have never met before

   - Two participants who work in different departments or organizations

   - Two participants who have different jobs, fields of study, or levels of knowledge or experience

   - Two participants whom you know share similar ideas and expectations for the project you are working on

   - Two participants whom you know have radically different ideas on the project

2. Ask the pairs to spend 30 to 60 minutes getting to know one another. Suggest that they go for a walk or have coffee together.

    If physically possible and relevant, suggest that they visit one another's workplace or office. If not, ask them to sketch and describe their own workplace in some detail.

3. Supply some questions that the pairs can use to interview one another, such as:

    - *Why have you come to this meeting?*
    - *What do you hope we accomplish?*
    - *What do you regard as the most important part of your job?*
    - *What do you like best about your job? What do you like least about it?*
    - *Describe your unit, department, organization, or agency.*
    - *What successes have you had? Accomplishments? What things do you feel good about having done on the job?*
    - *What problems do you encounter that are unique to you? Are probably shared by others?*
    - *What are your interests and hobbies?*
    - *If you weren't here today, what would you be doing that you're glad to put off?*

4. When the entire group reconvenes, give pairs a task to do together that enables them to contribute to the meeting.

5. Consider the appropriateness of forming the pairs into long-term learning partnerships. Remember that it is possible for a vice president and a job foreman to create a valuable alliance. It is also possible for the head of a manufacturing operation to learn from the sales director. For example, in a community group establishing a new museum, an interior decorator and the person overseeing costs could share their expertise to solve problems.

Variations

1. Have participants form trios or quartets instead of pairs.

2. Have participants introduce their partners to the entire group, giving a brief biographical sketch.

3. If you have a group that can handle things in a light-hearted way, ask the pairs to play True Confessions, during which each person divulges a single minor addiction or silly fear to the other, such as having a dish of ice cream every night, never missing "Xena, Warrior Princess" on television, or dreading rainy days or the coming of winter.

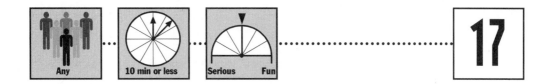

A Representative Sample

Overview

Sometimes, the group convening for a meeting is very large, and it is impossible to get a quick sense of who is attending. This procedure allows you to draw a representative sampling of the entire group and get to know these participants by interviewing them publicly.

Procedure

1. Explain that you would like everyone to have the opportunity to introduce himself or herself, but the task would consume too much time, given the size of the group.

2. Say that instead you will invite a small sample of participants who represent some of the diversity in the group to introduce themselves. Your hope is to obtain a "representative sample."

3. Mention some ways in which the participants might be diverse. Ask for a volunteer to be the first member of the "representative sample." When that person raises his or her hand, ask a few questions of the participant and learn about

his or her expectations, skills, job experience, background, opinions, and the like.

4. Having heard the responses of the first volunteer, ask for a second volunteer who is *different* in some respect from the first volunteer.

5. Continue calling on new volunteers (you decide how many) who are different from those who have previously been interviewed.

Variation

Arrange a table and chairs suitable for a panel discussion. Invite each member of the sample to join the panel after he or she has been initially interviewed. When the panel is complete, invite the remaining participants to ask additional questions of the panel.

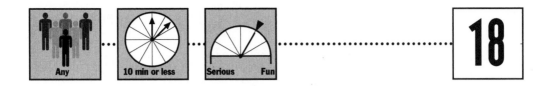

18

Stand Up and Be Counted

Overview

This a fast-moving way to acquaint the meeting participants with one another—especially in a large meeting.

Procedure

1. Explain to participants that you would like to conduct a quick survey to help everyone know "who's here today?"

2. Ask participants to *stand up and be counted* if a question you ask applies to them.

3. Develop questions that would be of interest from categories such as:

   - Occupation: ("Are there any social workers?")

   - Status: ("Who are the new members?")

   - Location: ("Who lives outside of the United States?")

   - Experience: ("Who has worked for this company for more than ten years?")

   - Beliefs: ("Who believes that no one has a right to commit suicide?")

- Opinions: ("Who thinks that we have been effective this year?")

- Preferences: ("Who drinks more than two cups of coffee a day?")

- Priorities: ("Who thinks it's important to spend more time on member recruitment than on program planning?)

4. Use anywhere from five to twenty-five polling questions. Remain within one of the above categories or mix them up. Do whatever will be of human interest to your participants. The activity works best if some of your questions will apply to virtually everyone and some will apply to just a few.

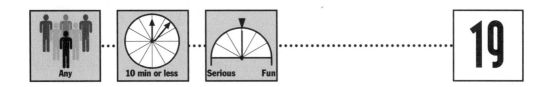

19

Introductory Go-Arounds

Overview

As a warm-up to any meeting, go-arounds are a way to capture briefly the thoughts and feelings that participants are bringing to the meeting. This process helps to open communication channels and bring hidden agendas to the surface. Go-arounds are also a participation equalizer that may set the tone for inclusion of every person attending the meeting.

Procedure

1. Explain to participants that you would like to begin the meeting by "going around" the group and hearing from everyone. Indicate that a sentence stem is useful in conducting go-arounds because each person can be brief and to the point.

2. Start at one end of the meeting table, or allow participants to share their endings whenever anyone feels like doing so. Invite participants to "pass" when it's their turn by saying, "I would prefer to pass" or "I pass *with dignity*." Also, invite participants to repeat what someone else has said previously if it expresses their sentiments as well. If you want, eliminate

repetition by asking each participant for a new contribution to the process. If the group is large, create a smaller go-around group by obtaining short responses from one side of the room, from people who are wearing glasses, or through some other sampling technique.

3. To surface thoughts and feelings about the meeting agenda, use one of the following stems:

   I hope this meeting. . . .

   By the end of this meeting,. . . .

   It's important today that we. . . .

   Briefly, my opinion about [insert topic] is. . . .

   I'm coming to this meeting. . . .

4. To elicit comments on a more personal level, use one of the following:

   I'm excited about. . . .

   Something that happened to me since the last time we met is that. . . .

   Some recent good/bad news I've had is. . . .

   Today I feel like. . . .

   I'm thankful that. . . .

   I'm looking forward to. . . .

5. To bring out feelings about the group or organization in general, use one of these:

   One thing I'm frustrated by is. . . .

   I just wish that. . . .

   I want to tell you. . . .

   I would prefer. . . .

   I am pleased that. . . .

Variation

Ask participants to take turns calling out words or phrases that come to mind when they think about "today's meeting," for example: *overdue, ambitious, exciting, tense, fun,* or *too short.* Record these free associations on the flip chart, allowing as much time for refection as possible and obtaining the most possible words. Then process by asking: *What does this list tell us about what's on our minds as we consider the upcoming meeting?*

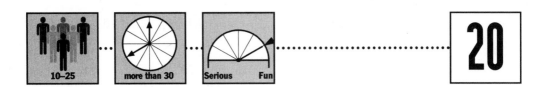

10-25 · more than 30 · Serious Fun

Team Getaway

Overview

Often, the work to be done at meetings can be done more effectively by creating long-term work teams. It helps to conduct some initial team-building activities to ensure a solid start. Although there are many possible team-building activities to consider, this one is a favorite of mine.

Procedure

1. Divide participants into team of three to six members. Give each team an equal number of index cards (different sizes in each stack are best).

2. Challenge each team to construct a model of a "getaway retreat" solely from the index cards. Team members can fold and tear the cards, but can use no other supplies for the construction.

3. Encourage teams to plan their retreats before they begin to construct them. Provide marking pens so that teams can draw on the cards and decorate the getaways as they see fit.

4. Allow at least 15 minutes for the construction. Do not rush or pressure the teams, as it is important for team members to have a successful experience.

5. When the construction work is finished, invite the entire group to take a tour of the getaway retreats. Visit each getaway and ask team members to show off their work and explain any special features of their retreats. Applaud each team's accomplishments. It is important not to encourage competitive comparisons among the constructions.

Variations

1. Ask the teams to build a team "monument" instead of a getaway retreat. Urge them to make the team monument sturdy, high, and aesthetically pleasing.

2. Call together the entire group and ask participants to reflect on the experience by responding to this question: "What were some helpful and not so helpful actions we did as a team and individually when working together?"

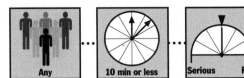

Reconnecting

Overview

If the project on which you're working involves a series of meetings stretching over a period of time, it is sometimes helpful to spend a few minutes "reconnecting" with participants after an absence. This strategy considers some ways to do this.

Procedure

1. Welcome participants back. Explain that you think it might be valuable to spend a few minutes becoming "reconnected" before proceeding with today's meeting.

2. Pose one or more of the following questions to the participants:

    - *"What do you remember about our last meeting? What stands out for you?"*

    - *"Have you had any afterthoughts about what we discussed at our last meeting?"*

    - *"What interesting experiences have you had between meetings?"*

- *"What's on your mind right now that might interfere with your ability to give full attention to today's meeting agenda?"*
- *"How do you feel today? Like a bruised banana? Or a crunchy apple?"*
- *"What 'good news' has happened to you since the last time we met?"*

3. Use any of the participation methods from "Ten Methods for Obtaining Group Participation" on page 17 appropriate to the size of your group and the amount of time you can allocate to the activity.

4. Segue to the topic of the current meeting.

Variations

1. Review the last meeting from notes, rather than posing questions.

2. Present two questions, concepts, or pieces of information covered in the previous meeting. Ask participants to vote for the one they would most like you to review.

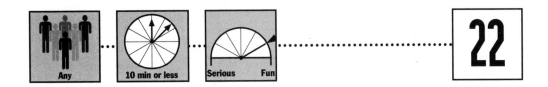

Lightening the Meeting

Overview

Creative humor can bring a potentially dull meeting to life right from the beginning. Humor also loosens people up and starts them thinking along different lines, so it can have a productive effect on the meeting outcome.

Procedure

1. Explain to participants that you want to do an enjoyable opening activity with them before getting serious about the meeting agenda.

2. Divide the participants into subgroups. Give them an assignment that asks them to make fun of an important topic or issue to be discussed in the meeting.

3. Some examples might be the following:

   • Brainstorm the best ways we can wreck this meeting.

   • Brainstorm the worst things we can do to our budget.

4. Invite subgroups to present their "creations." Applaud the results.

Variations

1. You can spoof the meeting agenda with a creation of your own making.

2. Create a multiple-choice pre-test on the meeting topics. Add humor to the answer choices for each item. Ask participants to select the answer for each question that they think could not possibly be right.

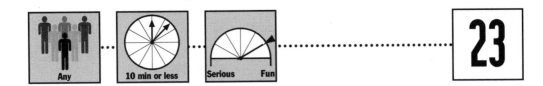

Getting in Sync with One Another

Overview

The need to work together is what brings people to a meeting in the first place. But working together isn't always easy. It requires skill, as well as a knowledge of one another's strengths and abilities and a little practice. The following quick activities will show dramatically how much people have to learn about one another to work well together. Participants will also discover how easy it can be if they accept the concessions and constraints working together requires.

Procedure

1. Tell the participants it might be fun to get in sync with one another and challenge them to sing a simple tune together without a leader. Hand out copies of the words for a familiar favorite. Then ask participants to sing the tune.

2. Challenge participants to create a group story. Have one participant begin by completing the sentence: "Once upon a time, there. . . ." Ask each subsequent participant to add one sentence to the story.

3. Pass out sound and rhythm instruments and ask the participants to try to make music together, or just have them clap the rhythm of a well-known song.

4. Pass a ball around the group and see whether they can do it more rapidly each time. Then introduce a second ball going in the opposite direction.

5. Have the participants pass an orange caught under the chin to the same area on the next person without using their hands. Continue around the group in the same way.

6. Have the participants line up in alphabetical order by their first names without talking. However, they have to find out the other people's first names in some manner.

7. Provide a selection of building blocks or Lego®s and ask one person to start a small structure with several blocks. Then ask each person to add just one block to the building project.

8. Try a fun-filled exercise called "Linking Up." Ask the participants to create a chain of paper clips with each person using only one hand.

Variations

If there is time, two more games are a lot of fun. Both provide much insight into the skills needed for working together.

1. "Find the Pruey" brings group members together and touching. Secretly designate one member of the group as the "pruey," but the person must keep his or her identity a secret. Tell other group members to station themselves around the room and keep their eyes closed. In order to find the pruey, the participants must circulate (with eyes closed) and continuously say, "Pruey, pruey." The pruey remains quiet, so if two people make contact by shaking hands and say the word "pruey" to each other, they must keep looking. When a group member does find the silent pruey, he or she continues

to hold the pruey's hand and also becomes silent. Each group member who makes contact with the expanding pruey stays with it and remains silent. Fewer and fewer people will be heard searching for the pruey, and the group will soon become one giant, silent pruey. Then all group members can open their eyes.

2. The "Rope Game" shows how a mix of participants' strengths and weaknesses can be used to reach goals. Up to nine people can play this game at one time. Blindfold the players and lead them to a nylon rope circle in a large room free of obstacles and tell them to hold onto the rope. Ask them to form a triangle. Natural leaders and followers become apparent as the group communicates and tries to form the shape. When they think they've completed the task, ask them to hold still and then take their blindfolds off so they can see how they fared. Then tell them to put their blindfolds back on and discreetly pull the leaders aside and tell them not to speak. That will usually force some of those who were followers to take up a leadership role. Discuss what happened after the game ends.

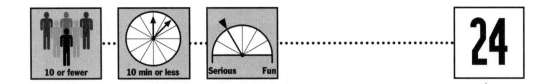

Clearing the Air

Overview

People often bring unvoiced worries and expectations to a meeting. Together, these concerns can actually impede progress, so it is very important to clear the air right at the beginning.

Procedure

1. In an informal discussion as the meeting begins, ask the participants what they want from this meeting and what they are prepared to give to it. Share your honest expectations for the meeting as well.

2. Other questions to ask may include all or any of the following:
   - *"What do you want from others?"*
   - *"What do you need to know about the agenda items?"*
   - *"What concerns do you have about the meeting?"*
   - *"What do you look forward to in this meeting?"*
   - *"What would make this meeting effective?"*

3. Another way to obtain answers to these or other questions is to ask the participants to write about their concerns and their wishes for the outcome of the meeting. Provide different colored index cards for each question and ask for short answers.

4. Collect the cards and group them according to similar responses. Address all concerns before the actual meeting begins.

Variation

A great way to clear the air in larger groups is to select a random group of "reporters" before the meeting begins and while people are still milling around. Assign each reporter to a group of eight people. Direct the reporters to interview the people in their groups to find out as much as possible about what is on the people's minds. Explain to the participants what you are doing and ask for their cooperation.

Reporters may want to ask the following questions:

- *"Why are you here and what do you expect from the meeting?"*
- *"Do you have any special goals you would like to share with the group?"*
- *"Do you have any doubts about the value of the meetings and the project to come?"*
- *"Is there a special part of the project that is dear to you? Why is that?"*

After the reporters have collected responses to these and any other pertinent questions, ask them to summarize their findings for the large group, but not to repeat information that other reporters have already presented.

Record the points the reporters make on a flip chart. Most people appreciate this sense of openness, and you can learn a lot from the concerns they have expressed.

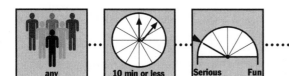

Agenda Review and Approval

Overview

An agenda that has been prepared in advance of a meeting should be reviewed and approved by participants before getting down to business. Sometimes, this is only a formality, but it's best to be ready with a process that will create the proper "buy-in" to the meeting.

Procedure

1. Inform the group that the meeting agenda you have prepared in advance is a road map that has been developed for the benefit of the group in achieving its goals. Say that you believe the more everyone knows about the goals of the meeting, the more effective the meeting will be. State emphatically that no effort has been make to advance the personal agenda of the meeting planners.

2. Further explain that you welcome questions and suggestions about the agenda, as well as participant consent to proceed. Explain that you have set a time limit for the process and that

you believe that adequate time is available for the agenda, if it meets the group's approval.

3. Distribute the agenda or ask participants to take out prior communications about it. Ask participants to *review* the agenda privately or in pairs before seeking clarification and approval. *Do not open discussion to the group yet.*

4. Poll the participants by asking them to raise their hands in response to the following questions:

   • *"Does anyone want clarification?"*

   • *"Does anyone have comments or suggestions?"*

5. Invite those seeking clarification to go first. Answer their questions (or have someone who is a better source of information do so). Hold off any in-depth discussion of agenda items.

6. Then proceed to obtain all comments and suggestions. It is usually better to hear all the comments briefly before responding. If suggestions can be easily incorporated, do so. If not, as facilitator, you must decide whether to spend the time seeking creative resolutions to the issues raised. Make this decision by weighing the importance of participant input against the need to proceed as planned. It is legitimate to set a question aside on a separate newsprint sheet if you are certain it will be answered in the course of the meeting.

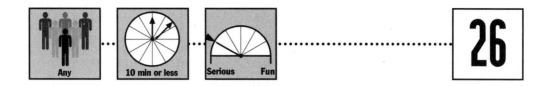

On-the-Spot Agenda Setting

Overview

The agenda should be set in advance when the group is large and/or does not meet on a regular basis. But setting an agenda at the beginning of a meeting is practical when the group is small, informal, and meets frequently. The advantage of this method is that every participant feels a part of the goal-setting process.

Procedure

1. Generate all the issues participants would like to discuss within the given period of time allotted for the meeting and write them on a flip chart.

2. Group items that can be combined.

3. Have participants rank each potential agenda item, considering the following:

   • How important the item is, given the group's priorities

   • How much time will be needed for discussion

   • How urgent the item is (that is, whether it can be postponed or is even important)

4. Select items that are ranked highest by the group (top half or fourth of the list) and estimate the time required for each one, including discussion, problem solving, and planning.

5. Order the highest ranking items, using these considerations:

   • Highest rank first

   • Flow of topics (It makes sense to discuss X before Y.)

   Try to avoid the trap of doing the easier, less time-consuming items first. You may never work on the important ones.

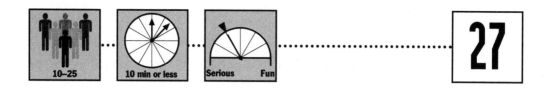

27

Beginning at the End

Overview

What makes many meetings humdrum affairs is that they feel like "business as usual," rather than "business as unusual." When members express their vision of what the group might accomplish, they create a climate of excitement and expectation. Try a process of "beginning at the end" to achieve this result.

Procedure

1. Ask participants to do a "thought experiment." They are to imagine that the meeting is over or the committee's work is completed. Imagine that a feeling of satisfaction permeates the room. The meeting has been successful and productive.

2. Display the question below and ask each participant to think about it:

   • *"What was the most important thing we accomplished today?"*

3. Pair up participants and ask them to share their answers with one another.

4. Next, ask the pairs to select one of their accomplishments (or combine them) to report to others.

5. Then ask each pair to write the result on an index card you provide. Have them give you the completed cards, reshuffle them, and hand out a new card to each pair.

6. Invite a member of each pair to read the card they received to hear an anonymous list of "What we want to accomplish at today's meeting." Write the list on the flip chart.

Variations

1. Invite participants to imagine they are reading an article about the meeting in the next day's paper. What might it say?

2. Have the pairs create drawings that express their hopes for the meeting. Make a gallery of the drawings.

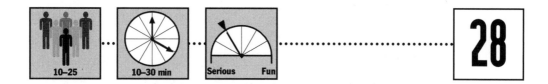

28

Setting Ground Rules

Overview

This is a way to let meeting participants set their own rules for behavior. When they feel a part of the process, they are more likely to follow the rules.

Procedure

1. Ask for a few volunteers (relative to the size of the group) to serve as "interviewers."

2. Have the interviewers circulate for a period of 10 to 15 minutes, making contact with as many people as time permits. Instruct the interviewers to ask group members the following question: "What behaviors do you think would be helpful or not helpful during this meeting?" (If necessary, first provide the group with some sample answers to guide their responses.)

3. At the end of the allotted time, ask the interviewers to report their findings back to the group. (If desired, list the findings on a flip chart or chalkboard.)

4. Usually, it is sufficient simply to hear the collected comments of the participants to establish a sense of the behavioral ground rules desired by the group. However, it is also possible to analyze the findings, look for overlap, and then consolidate the list. Post the list on the wall to remind everyone of the ground rules.

5. Invite participants to remind one another when a ground rule has been breached.

Variations

1. Provide a list of several possible ground rules. Ask participants to select three from the list. Tabulate the results. The following items might be suitable for your list:

   - Respect confidentiality.
   - Everyone participates when working in small groups or teams.
   - Observe the starting time of the meeting.
   - Get to know others different from yourself.
   - Let others finish what they are saying without interrupting.
   - No "put-downs" or "cheap shots"; focus on issues, not on people.
   - Speak for yourself.
   - Avoid squelching ideas prematurely.
   - No side conversations.
   - Be brief and to the point when speaking.
   - Use gender-sensitive language.
   - Be prepared for each meeting.
   - Do not sit in the same seat for every meeting.
   - Agree to disagree.

- Give everyone a chance to speak.
- Don't leave the meeting before it's over.

2. Have the group brainstorm ground rules for participation. Then use a procedure called "multi-voting" to arrive at a final list. Multi-voting is a method that reduces a list of items by one-half. Each participant votes on as many items as he or she wants; the half of the items with the highest number of votes remains on the list. (The procedure can be repeated as often as desired; each vote reduces the list by one-half.)

Stimulating Discussion, Dialogue, and Learning

Quality discussion, dialogue, and learning are crucial to the success of active meetings. When they are not present, any or all of the following may occur:

- Several participants are not engaged in the discussion.
- Comments are superficial and unfocused.
- Participants don't pay attention to one another.
- Some participants begin to dominate the group.
- The group goes off on unwanted tangents.
- Participants forget what they hear.

The nineteen strategies in this section all help to promote quality discussion, dialogue, and learning. Using some of them at your next meeting will go a long way toward improving the flow and retention of information and building excitement about new ideas and directions.

These strategies are ideal for agenda items for which information needs to be transmitted and reacted to. They are also useful when you want the group to discuss new business or reopen old business for further review.

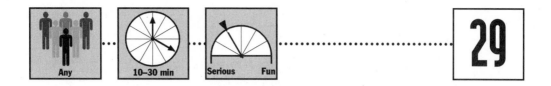

29

Town Meeting

Overview

Although this discussion format will work with any group size, it is especially well suited for large groups. By creating an atmosphere akin to a "town meeting," you can help the entire group to become involved in the discussion.

Procedure

1. Select one or several aspects of the material the participants will be considering. Briefly present the topic as objectively as you can, offering background information and an overview of different viewpoints. If you wish, provide documents to back up what you say.

   For example, this format worked well at a meeting called for the express purpose of obtaining input from various department heads on a company's hiring process. The company had hired a number of technical people who did not "fit" their new jobs. The company's chairman needed to decide whether the human resource department should continue to recruit and hire workers for technical positions or whether that process should be turned over to a specialized recruiting firm that had more expertise in screening and placing technical people.

2. Point out that you would like to obtain the participants' views on the matter at hand. Explain that, instead of calling on each participant, you will be following a format entitled "call on the next speaker." Whenever someone is finished speaking, that person should look around the room and call on someone else who also wishes to speak. When a person wants to speak, he or she should raise a hand.

3. Urge participants to keep their remarks brief so that as many others as possible can participate in the town meeting. Establish a time limit, if you wish, for the length of a speaker's turn. Direct participants to call on someone who has not previously participated before choosing someone who has already spoken.

4. Continue the discussion as long as it seems to be of value.

Variations

1. Organize the meeting into a debate. This method is particularly valuable if there is a clear-cut division of opinion over a specific topic. It's a good way to bring that out into the open. Invite participants to sit on one side of the room or the other, depending on their positions on the controversy. Follow the call-on-the-next-speaker format, but insist that the next speaker must have an opposing point of view. Encourage participants to move to the other side of the room if their views are swayed by the debate. Consider adding a third group of people who are "on the fence." Use the rule that participants cannot comment until they "get off the fence."

2. Begin the town meeting with a panel discussion. Have the panelists present their views and then use a call-on-the-next-speaker format to obtain audience reactions.

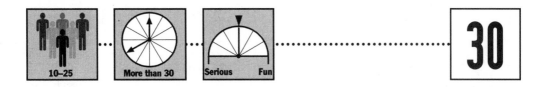

30

Three-Stage Fishbowl Discussion

Overview

A fishbowl is a discussion format in which a portion of the group forms a discussion circle and the remaining participants form a listening circle around the discussion group. This is one of the more interesting ways to set up a discussion.

Procedure

1. Devise three questions for discussion relevant to the meeting. Ideally, the questions should be interrelated, but that is not necessary. Decide in what order you would like the questions presented.

   For example, perhaps you are chairman of a committee planning a commemorative community fountain. The fountain project has faced unexpectedly severe criticism from some quarters, and you expect a lively debate. First, you probably would want to decide where the memorial fountain should be located. Next, you would want to decide on the general design of the fountain and then consider what the cost should be and how to pay for it.

2. Arrange chairs in a fishbowl configuration (two concentric circles). Have the participants count off by 1's, 2's, and 3's. Ask those from Group 1 to sit in the discussion circle and ask Groups 2 and 3 to take their places in the outer-circle seats. Pose your first question for discussion and allow up to 10 minutes for discussion. If you wish, ask one of the participants to lead the discussion.

3. Next, invite the members of Group 2 to sit in the inner circle, replacing Group 1 members, who now move to the outer circle. Ask the members of Group 2 whether they would like to make any brief comments about the first discussion, and then segue into the second discussion topic.

4. Follow the same procedure with members of the third discussion group.

5. When all three questions have been discussed, reconvene the group. Ask the participants for their thoughts about the entire project.

Variations

1. If it is not possible to have circles of chairs, have a rotating panel discussion instead. One third of the group serve as panelists for each discussion question. The panelists can sit in front of the room facing the rest of the participants. If you are using a U-shaped arrangement or a conference table, designate a side of the table for the panel group.

2. Use only one discussion question rather than three. Invite each subsequent group to respond to the discussion of the preceding group.

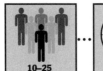

10–25   10–30 min   Serious   Fun

31

Expanding Panel

Overview

This activity is an excellent way to stimulate discussion and active participation while giving participants an opportunity to identify, explain, and clarify issues.

Procedure

1. Select a meeting issue sure to engage the participants' interests. Present the issue so that participants will be stimulated to discuss their viewpoints. Identify five questions for discussion.

   For example, a group of managers meets regularly to discuss methods of increasing productivity. Some believe allowing workers to telecommute is a viable option; others strongly oppose that step. Some probable questions could be:

   - *"What does telecommuting offer the company?"*
   - *"How complicated would it be to set up and equip a telecommuting program?"*
   - *"Will the initial cost be offset by later savings for the company?"*

- *"Are certain jobs more likely to be suitable for a telecommuting program? If so, which ones?"*
- *"Should workers be allowed to volunteer to telecommute or should managers select them?"*

2. Choose four to six people to serve as a panel discussion group. Ask them to sit in a semicircle at the front of the room.

3. Ask the remaining participants to position themselves on three sides of the discussion group in a horseshoe arrangement.

4. Begin with a provocative opening question. Moderate a panel discussion with the core group while the observers take notes in preparation for their own discussions.

5. At the end of the designated discussion period, separate the entire group into subgroups to continue with a discussion of the remaining questions.

Variations

1. Reverse the sequence; begin with small-group discussion and follow with a panel discussion.

2. Invite the participants to generate the questions for discussion.

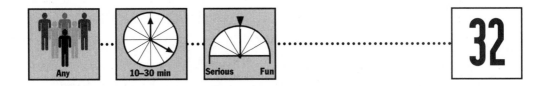
Point-Counterpoint

Overview

This activity is an excellent technique to stimulate discussion and gain a deeper understanding of complex issues. The format is similar to a debate, but is less formal and moves more quickly.

Procedure

1. Select an issue that has two or more sides.

   For example, the former chairman of the board of a company that employs about five hundred people has died and left a large sum in his will for a project to be selected by the employees. Workers are sharply divided between building a fully equipped fitness center and setting up an on-site library for employees. Compelling arguments have been offered for each project.

2. Divide the participants into subgroups according to the number of positions that have been stated. Ask each subgroup to come up with arguments to support its position. Encourage subgroup members to work with partners or in small cluster groups.

3. Reconvene the entire group, but ask members of each subgroup to sit together with space between the subgroups.

4. Explain that any participant can begin the debate. After that participant has had an opportunity to present one argument in favor of his or her assigned position, allow a different argument or counterargument from a member of another subgroup. Continue the discussion, making sure that all positions are presented.

5. Conclude the activity by summarizing and comparing the different positions. Allow for follow-up reactions and discussion.

Variations

1. Instead of holding a full-group debate, pair up individual participants from different subgroups and have them argue with one another. This can be done simultaneously, so that every participant is engaged in the debate at the same time.

2. Line up two opposing subgroups so that they are facing each other. As one person concludes his or her argument, have that participant then toss an object (such as a ball or a beanbag) to a member of the opposing side. The person catching the object must rebut the previous person's argument.

33

Feedback Teams*

Overview

Meetings often have presentations of information. This activity is a way to help participants stay focused and alert during a meeting presentation and to promote discussion afterward.

Procedure

1. Divide the participants into four teams and give the teams these assignments:

Team	Role	Assignment
1.	*Questioners*	After the presentation, ask at least two questions about the information presented.
2.	*Agreers*	After the presentation, tell which points your team agreed with (or found helpful) and explain why.

---

*Based on a strategy developed by Rebecca Birch and Cynthia Denton-Ade.

3.   *Nay Sayers*   After the presentation, comment on which points your team disagreed with (or found unhelpful) and explain why.

4.   *Example Givers*   After the presentation, explain specific examples or applications of the material.

2. After the information has been presented, give the teams a few moments to complete their assignments.

3. Call on each team to question, agree, disagree, or give examples.

Variation

Use only one assignment instead of four. For example, each team could be asked to be questioners.

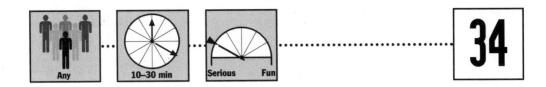
I Have a Question

Overview

The process of learning something new is more effective if the participant is in an active, searching mode, rather than in a passive mode. One way to create the active-learning mode is to stimulate participants to delve into subject matter on their own without prior explanation from the presenter and then let them generate questions to pose to the presenter. This simple strategy allows the presenter to feed off participants' questions, rather than give a "canned" presentation.

Procedure

1. Distribute to participants a handout outlining some of the points to be addressed. Key to your choice of handouts is the need to stimulate questions from the participants. A handout that provides broad information but lacks details or explanatory backup material is ideal. An interesting chart or diagram that illustrates some aspect of the issue is a good choice. A summary that is open to interpretation is another good possibility. The goal is to evoke curiosity.

For example, say you chair a large environmental group currently upset over a plan to quarry rock at a former toxic waste site. Group members are so emotionally caught up in this issue that they are making ridiculous claims that could damage the organization's reputation. You need to teach them quickly and thoroughly exactly what the underlying issues are.

2. Ask participants to study the handout with a partner. Request that the partners make as much sense of the handout as possible and that they place question marks next to information they do not understand. Encourage participants to insert as many question marks as they wish. If time permits, form the pairs into quartets and allow time for each pair to help the other.

3. Reconvene the group and answer participants' questions. In essence, the presentation will be directed by the group's questions rather than by a preset speech. Or, if you wish, listen to all the questions first and then proceed with a planned presentation, making a special effort to respond to the questions posed by participants.

Variations

1. If you feel that participants will be lost trying to study the material entirely on their own, provide some additional information to help guide them in their inquiries. Then proceed with the study groups.

2. Begin the procedure with individual study rather than pair study.

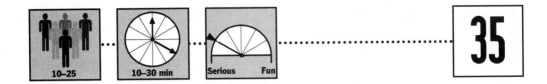

35

The Study Group

Overview

This method gives participants the responsibility to study information and to clarify its content as a group instead of merely listening to a presenter. The study assignment needs to be specific enough so that the resulting study session will be effective and so that the group will be able to be self-managing.

Procedure

1. Give participants a short, well-formatted handout covering meeting material—a brief text or an interesting chart or diagram. Ask them to review it silently. The study group will work best when the material is moderately challenging or open to widespread interpretation.

   For example, this method could be effective for the type of meeting necessary when a company draws all its top-level managers together to review the possibility of reorganizing its operations. Participants would need to review details of the present structure, but also would require information on alternate ways of running businesses and their pros and cons before they could speak intelligently on the issue.

2. Form subgroups of three to six members and give them a quiet space to conduct their study sessions.

3. Provide clear instructions that guide participants to study and explicate the material carefully. Include directions such as the following:

   • Clarify the content.

   • Create examples, illustrations, or applications of the information or ideas.

   • Identify points that are confusing or with which you disagree.

   • Argue with the text; develop an opposing point of view.

   • Assess how well you understand the material.

4. Assign jobs such as facilitator, timekeeper, recorder, or spokesperson to subgroup members.

5. Reconvene the entire group and do one or more of the following:

   • Review the material together.

   • Check for any questions.

   • Ask participants to assess how well they understand the material.

   • Provide an application exercise for participants to solve.

Variations

1. Do not form subgroups. Create a full-group study session. Read the material aloud. Stop the reading to answer participants' questions, to pose questions of your own, or to expound on the material.

2. If the group is large enough, create four or six study groups. Then combine parts of study groups and ask them to compare notes and help one another.

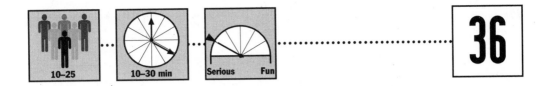

36

Group to Group Exchange

Overview

This is another way to avoid one-way meeting presentations. In this strategy, different information is given to different subgroups of participants. Each subgroup then "teaches" what it has learned to the rest of the group.

Procedure

1. Select a topic that promotes an exchange of information. Examples of topics include the following:
   - Three new products
   - Different ways to improve employee performance
   - Safety procedures
   - Two new policy recommendations
2. Divide the participants into as many subgroups as there are subtopics. In most cases, two to four subgroups are appropriate for this activity. Provide each subgroup with appropriate background information on the selected topic. Give each subgroup up to 30 minutes to create a presentation for the

assigned topic viewpoint. For example, if the topic were safety, one subgroup might present information about ways to reduce workplace accidents and a second subgroup might present information about a new security system.

3. When the preparation phase is completed, ask each subgroup to select a spokesperson. Invite each spokesperson to address the other subgroup(s).

4. After a brief presentation, encourage participants to ask questions of the presenter or to offer their own views. Allow other members of the spokesperson's subgroup to respond.

5. Continue the remaining presentations until each subgroup has expressed its views and has responded to audience questions and comments. Then compare and contrast the information that was exchanged.

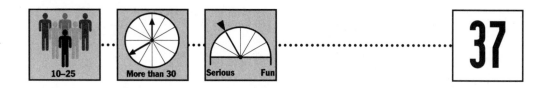
Jigsaw Discussion

Overview

"Jigsaw Discussion" is similar to "Group to Group Exchange," with one important difference: Every single participant is a presenter. It is an exciting alternative whenever there is a topic to be discussed that can be segmented or "chunked." Each participant learns something that, when combined with the material learned by others, forms a coherent body of information for discussion.

Procedure

1. Choose material that can be broken into segments. A segment can be as short as one sentence or as long as several pages. (If the material is lengthy, ask participants to read their assignments before the meeting.) Examples of appropriate material include the following:

   - Charts and graphs
   - A series of reports
   - A multi-point handout
   - A text that has different sections or subheadings

- A list of definitions
- A group of magazine-length articles or other kinds of short reading material.

For example, XYZ Manufacturing Company is considering purchasing a piece of computer-operated machinery that would demand many changes within the firm's production operation. One group might be assigned to look at data on the cost-effectiveness of the move; a second group would look into whether retooling would be required for other equipment; still another would read a plan for reassigning or reducing personnel; and a fourth might study a suggested timeline for the process of purchasing and placing the machinery on-line.

2. Count the number of information segments and the number of participants. In an equitable manner, give out different assignments to different subgroups. For example, imagine a group of twelve. Assume that you can divide materials into three segments or "chunks." You might then be able to form quartets, assigning each group segment 1, 2, or 3. Then ask each quartet or "study group" to read and discuss the material assigned to them. (If you wish, you can form participants into pairs or "study buddies" first and then combine the pairs into quartets.)

3. After the study period, form "cooperative learning" subgroups that contain a representative of every study group at the meeting. In the example just given, the members of each quartet could count off 1, 2, 3, or 4 and then form cooperative learning subgroups with participants who had the same number. The result would be four trios. In each trio one person would have studied segment 1, one would have studied segment 2, and one would have studied segment 3. The following diagram displays this sequence.

Total Group Explanation

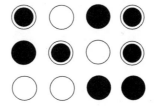

Study Group

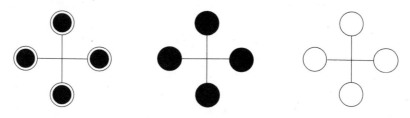

Cooperative Learning Groups

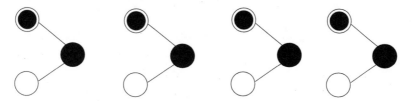

Diagram reproduced from *20 Active Training Programs*, Vol. II by Mel Silberman, S. Jullierat, K. Lawson, & N.C. Lewine. Copyright © 1994 by Jossey-Bass/Pfeiffer, San Francisco, CA.

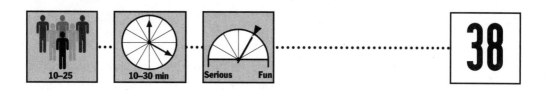

38

Card Exchange*

Overview

This is a clever strategy to help a medium to large group of people share ideas and opinions about issues that concern them.

Procedure

1. Before the meeting starts, prepare several index cards on which you have written some statements about a major issue facing the group. Prepare as many cards are there are participants, and hold them in reserve.

   For example, the following statements might be made about the financial difficulties facing an organization:

   - *We waste money by sending out unnecessary mailings.*
   - *Debt is normal, natural, and necessary for any growing organization.*
   - *We don't keep to our budget.*
   - *Our cash flow in the next four months will be better.*

---

*Based on a strategy developed by Sivasailam "Thiagi" Thiagarajan.

2. Hand out two blank cards to each participant on which you ask them to write brief statements about the issue you have chosen. Encourage them to be honest. Explain that their answers will be anonymous.

3. Collect the cards and shuffle them well with your prepared cards. Then randomly distribute to each participant three cards. Tell them to examine the cards and to arrange them in order of importance. Then instruct them to mill around the room exchanging cards in order to obtain a set of three they are in agreement with. Call time after 5 minutes. (If some participants complain about the cards they presently hold, tell them: "Relief is on the way.")

4. Arrange people in trios and have them select the three cards they prefer as a group. Ask them to discard cards they do not want and place them in a spot accessible to the other trios. Any trio can rummage through the discarded cards to find any they prefer over the ones they have. Call time after 10 minutes.

5. Invite each group to give a short report on the statements they have chosen. (Consider giving each trio a sheet of newsprint and some markers to display their chosen statements.)

6. Have the entire group reflect on the commonalties and diversity of viewpoints among the subgroups.

Variation

This process can also be used to generate and discuss suggestions for change, factors that may be creating problems, or creative ideas for new initiatives.

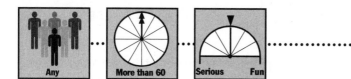

39

Snowball Discussion

Overview

This strategy is a classic way to build dialogue, especially in a large group. Discussion begins in pairs, then quartets, and then octets, and so forth (depending on the size of the group). It requires open space and chairs that can be easily moved.

Procedure

1. Introduce any discussion question appropriate to your group. For example, a group planning its annual conference might be asked: "How can we make our annual conference special this year?"

2. Explain the "snowball discussion" design. Pair up participants and ask them to discuss the question for 5 minutes.

3. Ask pairs to form quartets. (If there is an odd pair, have them join one of the quartets). Give them 10 minutes to exchange ideas. Ask each quartet to appoint a spokesperson.

4. Combine quartets into octets. (If there is an odd quartet, have them join one of the octets). Give them 20 minutes to hear

from each quartet spokesperson and react to the ideas given. Select a spokesperson to report on the octet discussion.

5. Finally, combine octets into groups of sixteen participants. Have each spokesperson give a report and than allow 40 minutes for discussion and closure.

Variations

1. Limit or extend the "snowball," depending on the size and time parameters of your meeting.

2. Conclude the snowball discussion with a panel discussion, drawing panelists from the spokespersons previously selected.

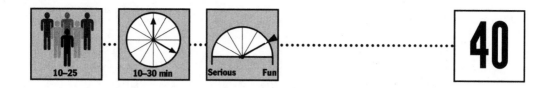

40

Go to Your Post

Overview

This is a fun way to incorporate physical movement into meeting discussions. It's great for a tired group and a surefire way to stimulate dialogue.

Procedure

1. Post signs around the room that say: "strongly agree," "agree," "not sure," "disagree," "strongly disagree."

2. Create statements on issues being considered by the group. For example:

   "I think we should spend more time on this issue."

   "I would like to make a change in [insert topic]."

   "We need to enlarge the committee."

   "We should make more of an effort to [insert action]."

3. Read the first statement. Ask participants to move to the place in the room where their feeling about the statement is posted.

4. Have the subgroups that have been created discuss among themselves why they have chosen to be where they have placed themselves. Ask a representative of each group to summarize the reasons for the total group.

5. Continue to read other statements and repeat the process, with participants moving as desired.

Variations

1. Pair up participants with different preferences and ask them to compare their views or create a discussion panel with representatives from each preference group.

2. Ask each preference group to make a presentation, create an advertisement, or prepare a skit that advocates their viewpoints.

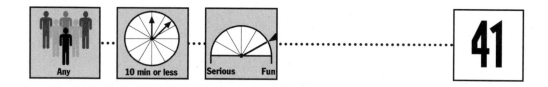

Instant Assessment*

Overview

This is an enjoyable, nonthreatening technique to stimulate discussion. It is similar to "Go to Your Post" but moves more quickly and does not require physical movement.

Procedure

1. Create a set of "responder" cards for each participant. These cards could contain the letters A, B, or C for multiple choice questions, or Agree and Disagree, or numerical ratings such as 1 through 5.

2. Develop a set of statements that participants can respond to by using their cards. The following are some sample statements:

   I think we should:
   A. *Stop the project.*
   B. *Continue the project as is.*
   C. *Make modifications to the project.*

   We are taking on more than we can handle. Agree or Disagree?

*Based on a strategy developed by Rebecca Birch and Cynthia Denton-Ade.

On a five-point scale ("1" is "not important" and "5" is "very important"), rate how important it is to you to develop a mission statement.

3. Read the first statement and ask participants to respond by holding up the card of their choice.

4. Quickly assess the response. Invite a few participants to share the reasons for their choices.

5. Continue with the remaining statements.

Variations

1. Instead of using cards, ask participants to stand when their choice is announced.

2. Use a conventional show of hands, but add interest by encouraging participants to raise both hands when they strongly agree with a response.

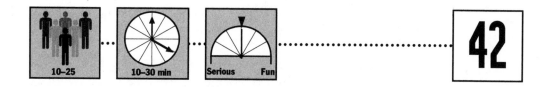

42

Rotating Trios

Overview

This is an in-depth way for participants to discuss issues with some (but usually not all) of their fellow participants. Participants are placed in a series of subgroup discussions with different people.

Procedure

1. Compose a variety of questions that will help participants begin discussion of an agenda item.

2. Divide participants into trios. Position the trios in the room so that each trio can clearly see a trio to its right and to its left. (The best configuration of trios is in a circle or square.)

3. Give each trio an opening question (the same question for each trio) to discuss. Select the least threatening question you have to begin the trio exchange. Suggest that each person in the trio take a turn answering the question.

4. After a suitable period of discussion, ask the trios to assign a 0, 1, or 2 to each of their members. Direct the participants

with the number 1 to rotate one trio clockwise and the participants with the number 2 to rotate two trios clockwise. Ask the participants with the number 0 to remain seated. They will be permanent members of a trio site. Have them raise their hands high so that rotating participants can find them. The result of each rotation will be entirely new trios.

5. Start each new exchange with a new question. Increase the difficulty or sensitivity of the questions as you proceed.

6. Rotate trios as many times as you have questions to pose and the discussion time to allot. Use the same rotation procedure each time. For example, in a trio exchange of three rotations, each participant will meet six other participants for in-depth discussion.

Variations

1. After each round of questions, quickly poll the participants about their responses before rotating individuals to new trios.

2. Use pairs or quartets instead of trios.

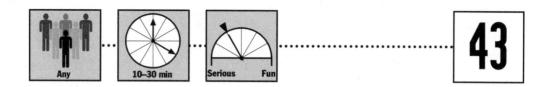

43

Anonymous Comments

Overview

This strategy enables participants to consider one another's views without holding a public discussion. Instead, they write down their comments and exchange them anonymously.

Procedure

1. Hand out a blank index card to each participant.

2. Ask the participants to write on the cards any comments they have about a particular issue facing the group. Encourage them to be brief and to write legibly because others will read what they write. Tell them not to put their names on the cards.

3. Request that the cards be passed around the group in a clockwise direction. As each card is passed on to the next person, he or she should read it and place a check mark on the card if it contains a comment he or she can support.

4. When a participant's card comes back to him or her, all other members of the group will have reviewed all of the cards and made check marks in support of the comments. At this point,

identify the comments that received the most affirmative votes (checks).

5. Invite some participants to share their comments, even if their cards did not receive the most check marks.

Variations

1. If the group is too large to take the time to pass the cards to all participants, break the group into subgroups and follow the same instructions. Or simply collect the cards at some point before everyone has seen them and respond to a sample of them.

2. Instead of writing their comments on the index cards, ask participants to write down their proposals, questions, and so forth and then pass them around.

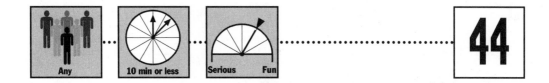

44

Active Opinion Sharing

··

Overview

For this strategy, participants complete a brief survey of their views and then share them with fellow participants.

Procedure

1. Create a list of survey questions pertaining to the agenda items of the meeting. Use formats such as sentence stems, multiple choice, rating scales, and short answers (as in the examples on the next page).

2. Distribute the survey and ask participants to complete it.

3. Then invite the participants to mill around the room, finding others who have answers that they themselves do not have. Encourage participants to exchange views.

4. Reconvene the full group and review the survey as a total group.

1. One way to increase accountability is. . . .
2. I think our programs have been:
   a.   too long
   b.   too short
   c.   just right
3. Our policy on patient eligibility needs to be reconsidered.

1	2	3	4	5
Strongly Agree	Agree	Not Sure	Disagree	Strongly Disagree

4. What one step should we take to improve customer service?

Variation

Rather than milling around, have participants form small groups to discuss their responses.

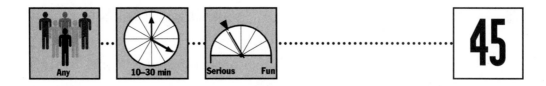

45

Meet the Press

Overview

Often outside experts or guest speakers at a meeting have little knowledge of the group to whom they are speaking. When it is time for "questions and answers," the audience is silent, confused, or annoyed. Consider turning the session into a form of "Meet the Press."

Procedure

1. Invite a speaker who is an expert on a subject of importance to your group. (For example, a loan officer could be the guest speaker for a group of bank customer-service representatives.)

2. Prepare the speaker ahead of time by telling him or her that the session will be conducted like a press conference. In keeping with that format, the speaker will make a few brief remarks and then answer questions from "the press" (the meeting participants).

3. Prior to the guest's appearance, prepare the participants by discussing how a press conference is conducted and then

giving them an opportunity to formulate several questions to ask the speaker.

Variation

Choose to have several guests at the same time and conduct round-table discussions. Seat each speaker at a table or in a circle of chairs to share information and experiences with a small group. The group members will have an opportunity to interact with the expert by asking questions in a more personal environment. Divide the session into a series of rounds. Determine the length of each round, depending on the time available for the session and the number of guests. In general, 10 or 15 minutes for each round is appropriate. Direct each small group to move from one expert to the next as the rounds progress.

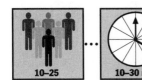

Everyone Is an Expert Here

Overview

At meetings, there is often a glut of opinion giving and a scarcity of information seeking. For this strategy, participants are coaxed into asking questions of one another.

Procedure

1. Hand out an index card to each participant. Ask participants to write down a question they have about a specific topic they would like discussed. It may be a question that requires expert information or an informed viewpoint. Here are some examples:

   - *"In your opinion, what will the cost of this project be?"*
   - *"Do we have to worry about obtaining a certificate of occupancy for our new building?"*

2. Collect the cards, shuffle them, and distribute one of them to each participant.

3. Invite participants to take turns reading aloud the question cards they have received and invite replies from others. Tell

the readers of the questions that they are also free to give any expert information or informed viewpoint they possess.

4. Make note of questions that have been left unanswered and discuss with the group how they would obtain an answer or whether one is necessary.

Variations

1. Form subgroups after the cards are redistributed. Each subgroup can examine the cards of its members and respond to them.

2. Ask participants to write down on cards an opinion rather than a question. After the cards are collected, shuffled, and redistributed, invite participants to agree or disagree with the opinions as they are read aloud.

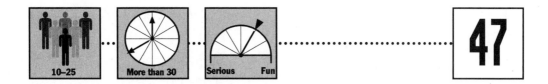

47

The Talking Stick[*]

Overview

"The Talking Stick," an ancient technique, also used in the past few centuries by Native Americans, helps participants focus on direct and honest communication in a way that permits everyone to speak on an equal basis. The technique was especially effective in tribal councils when controversial issues or serious conflicts had to be resolved. The stick, made by the council leader, or by the entire tribe, was a symbol of oneness, not only signifying the importance of the meeting and the commitment of the people, but also allowing equal time for all and regulating each speaker's behavior.

Procedure

1. Set aside some time for participants to make a talking stick. You may provide the bits and pieces required or ask participants at an earlier meeting to bring them in. The talking stick may be as simple as an unadorned twig from a tree, or as elaborate as you like, with glued or tied-on ornamentation

---

*Based on a strategy developed by Cindy Lindsay and Janis Pasquali.

such as feathers and beads and ribbons. The stick must be small enough to hold in one hand. Tell those at the meeting to consider the stick a physical symbol of the group's commitment to work together in a meaningful way.

2. Call together the participants and have them sit in a circle.

3. Explain the basic rules of the process:

    • Only the person holding the stick is permitted to speak.

    • He or she must speak briefly and to the point.

    • Speakers must tell the truth without judging or blaming others.

    • Listeners must do the same.

    • If a person has nothing to say when the stick is passed, he or she may simply pass it on to the next person.

    • The speaker may finish his comment by proclaiming "ho" to show that the rules of speaking and listening have been observed.

    • Participants may also affirm that with another "ho."

    • The stick may be passed from person to person in a clockwise direction or placed in the center of the circle for retrieval by the next person who wishes to speak.

4. You may determine whether you want the stick to be passed only once or whether it should continue around the circle with participants building on the last person's comments.

5. Decide when there has been enough discussion; then ask the participants to try to determine a common ground while still respecting differences of opinion.

6. After they have done this, you may summarize the outcome of the meeting for them and together decide on the next move to be made.

Variations

1. Make the talking stick yourself before the meeting if the group is pressed for time, but you probably will find that the participants will show more respect for the process and the outcome if they work on it as a group project.

2. This exercise has endless variations. You may conduct it inside or outside. You may go as "native" as you wish, depending on your assessment of the group's expectations and reactions to the technique.

3. Some facilitators bring the group together by grounding themselves in terms of the earth and even orient themselves to sun or stars or compass points.

4. Native musical instruments and drums make the technique more fun and even more memorable, and you may want to serve herbal tea to create real atmosphere.

Facilitating Creative Problem Solving

Whenever obvious solutions exist for problems under discussion, the hard part is over and the group can get down to planning how to implement those solutions. Often, however, the group is stuck for creative ideas and needs your facilitation help to get them over the hump. This section contains fifteen strategies to help promote creative problem solving at your meetings.

Many of the strategies involve well-known techniques such as brainstorming—but with many new twists. Using these techniques, your group members will have fun and, at the same time, challenge themselves to "get out of the box" and develop truly novel ideas.

It's important to explain the procedures carefully when doing these techniques for the first time. Participants are accustomed to saying whatever is on their minds, without thinking about how their comments affect the group's creative thinking process. Reminding them to stay within the boundaries of the processes you are using will help the group to find out how useful these techniques can be.

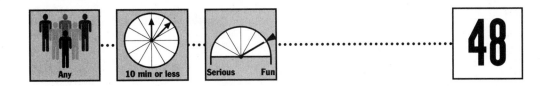

48

Creative Warmups

Overview

A group's creativity is fostered by thinking "outside the box"—looking at issues in new ways and developing novel solutions to problems. To go beyond the same tried-and-true ideas, it is helpful to warm up participants before launching into the real business of the group. There are a number of ways to help the brain become limber and ready for serious creative problem solving.

Procedure

1. Tell participants that you thought it might be fun to have a short warmup before doing some serious creative problem solving.

2. Select one or more of the following warm-up activities:

   Think of as many **uses** (even crazy ones) as you can for any of the following:

ruler	sticky note	belt	necktie
brick	pencil	sponge	aluminum can

Of course, the possible objects are endless, so brainstorm some others.

Think of **novel ways** to do the following:

peeling a navel orange	*simplifying your life*
holding a meeting	*greeting someone "hello"*
traveling from	*baking a pie*
coast to coast	

Think of as many **similes** as you can, such as

A meeting is like a. . . .

Our organization is like a. . . .

This project is like a. . . .

A facilitator is like a. . . .

Think of as many **excuses** as you can for:

Being late to a meeting

Wearing socks that don't match

Running out of gas

"Bouncing" a check

Think of as many **names/titles** as you can for the following:

A book on effective meetings

A film about Michael Jordan

A bowling team

A cemetery

Think of as many **thought experiments** as you can, such as:

What might happen if no men attended this meeting?

What might happen if dogs could speak?

What might happen if everyone in the world prayed at some time today?

What might happen if most people had to work the night shift?

What might happen if computers were banned?

What might happen if there were snow on the ground year round where you live?

3. Choose a method of participation from the following possibilities:

- Private reflection
- Team competition
- Total group sharing

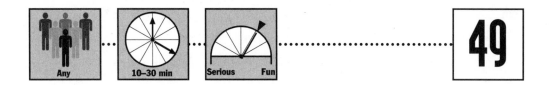

49

Fast and Slow Brainstorming

Overview

Brainstorming is a well-known technique to free the imagination to come up with new ideas about goals, projects, solutions, or whatever. Most people assume that brainstorming is a quick process of listing as many ideas as possible in a very short period of time. However, brainstorming can be done at a leisurely pace as well. Here are the two alternatives.

Procedure

1. *Fast brainstorming* can be compared to making popcorn. Kernels form in people's minds and out pop ideas (some of which may be "corny"). If things go well, you come up with a lot of ideas and then the list is exhausted. The process typically involves the following guidelines:

   - Participants are urged to *go for quantity.* The more ideas, the better.

   - Participants are encouraged to *think freely.* In some cases, the crazier the idea, the better.

- Participants are invited to *toss out* whatever occurs to them.
- Participants are required to *hold back any comments* about the ideas until the time for brainstorming is up.

As a result of the above, the pace is usually frenzied and uninhibited.

2. *Slow brainstorming* has a different tempo and feel. Participants are expected to be thoughtful and responsive. As a result, fewer ideas might be developed, but perhaps the quality will improve. However, there are still "rules" for this form of brainstorming:

- Participants are asked to *wait a few seconds* before shouting out their ideas.
- Participants are sometimes requested to *write down ideas first* before making them public.
- Participants are sometimes required to *limit themselves* to one contribution until everyone has either contributed or passed.
- Participants are urged to *ask clarifying questions.* When an idea is offered by someone, others are allowed to seek more information about the idea—as long as they don't make any judgment about the idea itself. For example, someone might ask: "How much do you estimate that will cost?" (in a friendly tone of voice), but could not ask (rhetorically): "Don't you think that's going to be expensive?"
- Participants are encouraged to *add to an idea* ("Maybe we could also. . . .").

3. The keys to either type of brainstorming session, fast or slow, are creative imagination and open, nonjudgmental interaction. Of course, after the ideas are produced—whether fast or slow—they must be listed, discussed, and evaluated.

4. One way to quickly sort out the participants' reactions to the brainstormed ideas is to group them into the following categories:

- Keepers (implement immediately)

- Maybes (promising enough to warrant serious consideration)

- Hold-offs (put aside for now)

Consider a method called "dot voting." Give participants sticky dots of different colors. Post the brainstormed ideas, designate one color for keepers, one color for maybes, and one color for hold-offs. Invite participants to come up to the list on the wall and evaluate each idea with a dot of the appropriate color. Survey the results and decide on actions that can be taken and who will undertake them.

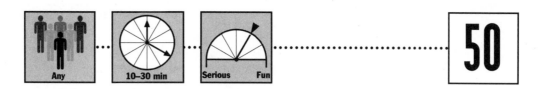

50

Brainwriting

Overview

Brainwriting is a quick and efficient way to draw out the best ideas from a group. It also levels the playing field in several ways. Brainwriting provides equal weight for each idea, whether it's suggested by the CEO or the janitor. In addition, it provides equal opportunity to play for both extroverts and introverts. Because the exercise is a written one, those who don't ordinarily speak up at a meeting often express themselves more freely. It also prevents ideas from being blocked, and perhaps lost, by those more articulate participants who tend to dominate with the spoken word.

Procedure

1. Hand out blank sheets of paper and ask each person to write on the paper just one idea concerning the program or project you're working on. It's important to stress to participants that the basic idea should be expressed in a phrase or two or in one sentence. Discourage lengthy suggestions.

2. Encourage participants to let their thoughts run free. Remind them that no idea is too silly to write down. Another person may see a practical way to implement the idea.

3. Participants should then pass their papers to the right.

4. Ask each participant to read the idea on the paper received and either try to build on that idea or use it to come up with an entirely new thought. Tell the participants to write their ideas just beneath the original ideas and again pass the paper to the person to the right.

5. Continue in the same way until each paper has a list of four or five ideas.

    For example, a team consulting group was brainstorming how to name its company. A person wrote on a card "Teams R Us." Someone followed with "Teams Rx." Next came "Prescriptions for Team Success" followed by "Team Doctors."

6. Have participants pass the sheets back to the person who wrote the original idea so he or she can see how others have built on it.

7. Ask the participants who wrote the original ideas to choose one or two of the best ideas from the sheet and discuss them with the group.

Variations

1. The sheets of paper can be passed to the left or to the front or back of a row, if participants are seated in that fashion.

2. If you are conducting a large meeting, separate the participants into work groups of five or six people and you'll collect even more ideas to discuss.

3. Brainwriting also can be effective when done via e-mail. It can even be extended to very large departments or an entire company, if it has an intranet.

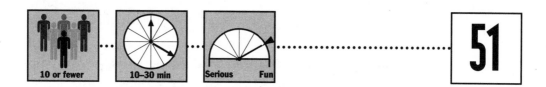

51

Brainwalking*

Overview

Brainwalking is based on the same principles as brainwriting, but it offers a more active, physical approach to the creative exercise. In brainwalking, the people circulate and the paper stays in place on the wall. Motion automatically increases energy, and seeing the lists of ideas posted also provides a sense of accomplishment for participants—even boosts more creative thinking.

Procedure

1. Before the meeting, tape individual sheets of large flip-chart paper on the walls of the meeting room.

2. Give participants felt-tipped markers in different colors. Be sure to select the brightest, boldest colors. (If you're using chalkboards or whiteboards instead, remember to provide colored chalk or erasable markers in various colors.) The colors will add excitement to the exercise, stimulate the participants, and make the final list of ideas look more interesting.

---

*Based on a strategy developed by Bryan Mattimore.

Tell participants to go to one of the sheets of paper on the wall and write down one idea about the meeting topic.

3. When they are finished, ask participants to move clockwise to the next paper and either build on the idea their predecessor has written or jot down a new idea not related to the original one.

4. Continue in the same direction until five or six people have written their ideas on each sheet.

5. Ask the participants to return to the sheet where they started and select one or two of the best ideas written there for discussion by the total group.

Variations

1. Set a more relaxed tone to the meeting by asking participants to draw their organization's symbol or company logo or a stick picture of their chairman or CEO. Or have them select one special word to describe the desired outcome of the meeting. The person declared "the winner," either by you, by acclamation, or however you choose, gets first choice of a wall position.

2. If the physical characteristics of the room prevent you from hanging anything on walls, provide large clipboards and lean them against the walls, place them on scattered chairs, or stand them at appropriate intervals so the participants have to move around.

3. You can brainwalk outdoors as well, which works well for a meeting in which participants have to be especially creative, such as coming up with a name for a new product line or the slogan for a sales campaign. Being outside also provides an added sense of freedom and you can simply hang clipboards or flip chart pages on trees or bushes.

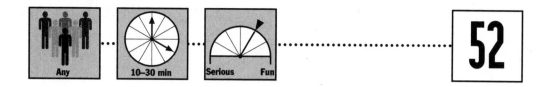

52

Part Changing

··

Overview

Often, brainstorming new ideas is difficult because the size of the problem taxes the creative imagination of the group. One way to overcome this situation is to break the problem, issue, or goal down into its constituent parts and examine each part separately. Then, participants can brainstorm ideas involving each part. Doing this will help to loosen up participants, and they may produce some truly novel and productive ideas.

Procedure

1. As the meeting begins, state the problem, issue, or goal about which you want to have a brainstorming session.

2. Next, ask the participants to think about all the elements or parts of the problem, issue, or goal by breaking it down. (Or do this analysis for them prior to the meeting.)

As an example, consider the planning of a successful fund-raising race. Here are some aspects of the project to be considered:

- *A slogan*

- *The course to be run*
- *A length for the race*
- *A date for the race (Is Saturday better than Sunday? Rain date or no? Maybe a holiday weekend?)*
- *Prizes*
- *A deadline for entries*
- *Emergency services*
- *Publicity, before, during, and after the race.*

3. Take each part of the problem and think about the alternatives. New ideas in each of the areas could be so powerful that next year's race could be a real winner, or it could change into a different kind of event, as a result of the planners looking at the project from a different perspective.

10–30 min

Serious   Fun

Brainstorming Roadblocks

Overview

For this technique, instead of asking participants how to achieve a goal, ask them instead what will block them from achieving their goal. Once these "roadblocks" are identified, have the group brainstorm how to overcome each obstacle, one at a time.

Procedure

1. Identify a goal that the group is having trouble attaining.

   For example, a business may be having difficulty attracting new accounts.

2. Then ask the group to list some of the reasons why it has been difficult to achieve its goal.

   Some factors that could be responsible for a business not obtaining new accounts may be increased competition, poor customer service, or diffuse marketing.

3. Explain that unless some or all of these roadblocks are overcome, the group will continue to face the same lack of success again.

4. Ask the group to start with one roadblock and brainstorm ways to overcome it. Suggest that the first roadblock might be worked on first for one of these reasons:

    - It is the key to eventual success.
    - It is the easiest place to start making changes.
    - It is something we can actually do something about.

5. Once a selection has been made, invite the group to brainstorm ways to overcome that obstacle.

6. Keep the group focused on removing one roadblock at a time. Groups usually become sidetracked when they try to handle too much at once.

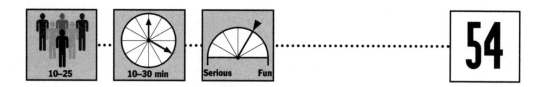

54

Negative Brainstorming*

Overview

We usually associate brainstorming with the notion of generating creative ideas to improve a situation or to achieve a desired outcome. This technique involves the opposite: brainstorming negative ideas to find positive ones.

Procedure

1. Identify a positive goal the group wants to achieve. Then reverse your thinking and think of its opposite. For example:

   • An inspiring mission statement is uninspiring.

   • A successful fund-raiser is a flop.

   • A streamlined process is complicated and inefficient.

   • A plan to improve customer satisfaction is a step backward.

2. Tell participants that you have a fun technique to release creative thinking. Present the brainstorming topic in the negative.

---

*Based on a strategy developed by Sivasailam "Thiagi" Thiagarajan.

For example, "What can we do to make . . .
- *our mission statement uninspiring?"*
- *our fund-raiser a flop?*
- *our process even more complicated and inefficient than it already is?*
- *a plan to upset customers?*

3. List the group's ideas on a flip chart.

4. Next, challenge the group to take as many of their "negative" ideas as they can and convert them to positive outcomes.

For example, someone might suggest that a surefire way to upset customers is to tell them that they are a source of annoyance. However, this negative behavior could be turned round by systematically telling customers to let you know at any time if there is anything you can do for them.

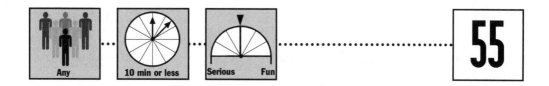

55

Clustering
Brainstormed Ideas

Overview

When a group has generated a number of ideas, it makes sense to first group the ideas into common clusters or themes before discussing each of them. Clustering ideas helps to build a team spirit because participants are looking for commonalties, not differences. The key is to develop a way to cluster ideas so that a group accepts the groupings that are created.

Procedure

1. One powerful method that can be used in a small-group setting is to do the clustering *silently.* Have participants write down ideas that have been brainstormed on index cards or sticky notes. Display the cards or notes randomly on a table, flip chart, or whiteboard. Invite participants to read the ideas that have been posted and then move the cards into groupings without speaking. (Allow participants to change the position of any card positioned by someone previously.) After all cards are grouped, have the participants agree on a label for each cluster.

2. Clustering *out loud* can be accomplished in these two ways:

- After brainstormed ideas have been posted on newsprint, ask participants how they can be grouped by asking:

  "Which ideas are similar to one another?"

  "Which ideas complement one another?"

  "Which ideas address the same issue or employ the same strategy?"

  Circle or underline common items with the same color marker or assign them the same letter. Doing so will create a visual display of how ideas cluster. Be sure to create a new list if the original becomes hard to decipher.

- Collect ideas on cards and shuffle the deck. Read each card, one at a time, and discuss whether any can be grouped with previously read cards. As the process unfolds, the cards will become organized into natural groupings.

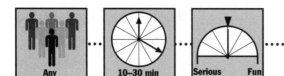

56

Looking at the Possibilities

Overview

This strategy employs a technique called "scenario thinking." Participants try to solve a problem creatively by setting aside present realities and dreaming up a wide range of new possibilities.

Procedure

1. Select an issue, problem, or creative project facing the group. For example, a group might be discussing employee morale, slackening attendance/participation, or customer service.

2. Tell the group members that you would like them to set aside their current concerns about "things the way they are" and to think about a range of future possibilities to resolve the issue, problem, or project by engaging in "scenario thinking." This is done by asking: "Can we look at it this way . . . and this way . . . and this way, and . . . ?"

3. Display one or more of the following sentence stems and say to participants: "Let's dream a little together. How could we expand our thinking about this?" Encourage participants to share their ideas beginning with the phrase(s):

- *I wonder. . . .*
- *What if. . . .*
- *Maybe we. . . .*
- *I have a dream that. . . .*
- *If only we. . . .*
- *I wish. . . .*
- *Why can't we. . . .*

4. Allow participants to speak whenever thoughts come to their minds. Encourage them to accept silences between contributions. Insist that people listen but not respond to what is shared until several statements have been made.

Variation

To inject humor and to loosen up a group, give each participant a pair of toy glasses that can be purchased from any party supply or children's toy store. Ask participants to wear them to help in "seeing new possibilities."

Wearing Someone Else's Shoes

Overview

Here is an idea to bring some creativity and fun to your meeting. Participants are asked to assume the identity of someone else in order to loosen their own thinking about an issue facing the group.

Procedure

1. Explain to participants that we often look at an issue from our own frame of reference. Sometimes, taking someone else's perspective casts a new light on the issue.

2. Identify an issue that your group is dealing with. For example, a nonprofit organization might be grappling with the development of a mission statement.

3. Give out cards to participants with role identities that are not their own. (Depending on the meeting size, each participant can receive a different identity, or two or more can share the same identity.) You might use categories such as:

customer	*board member*
community member	*top management*
student	*consultant*
volunteer	*competitor*
parent	*police officer*
teacher	*line worker*

Or ask participants to switch to a person of a different:

- Gender
- Age group
- Ethnic, religious, or racial background
- Region
- Personality type

Or you might choose well-known people. Here are some suggestions:

Bill Gates	*Martin Luther King*
Princess Diana	*Will Rogers*
Moses	*Toni Morrison*
Ted Turner	*Stephen Covey*
John Lennon	*Jane Austen*
Mark McGuire	*Harry Truman*

Or, if the participants know one another well, assign each participant the identity of someone else in the group.

4. Provide some way for each participant to show his or her assigned identity. Ask each participant to think about how the issue under consideration might look to the person whose identity he or she has assumed.

5. Request that participants discuss the issue "wearing someone else's shoes." Encourage them to really take on the iden-

tity of the person assigned to them. Continue the discussion for as long as it seems useful. Even 5 minutes might be enough time to shake participants from their own frames of reference and allow them to view things differently.

Variation

Consider providing costume items such as a hat, a sign, a pipe, a crown, and so forth to dramatize the process.

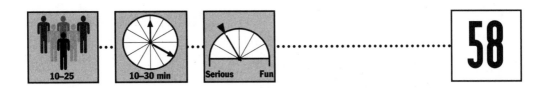

What's the Problem?

Overview

When trying to understand a problem, many "causes" or contributing factors are not obvious at first glance. Probing the problem for underlying or less obvious causes can be very fruitful. It gives a group an idea where to focus its creative efforts.

Procedure

1. Explain to participants that we often assume a problem we are facing has an easily explained cause. For example, if the last three projects were finished well past their deadlines, it must be that we don't have enough project delivery resources in place. By focusing on this as the cause, many other ways to look at the problem may be hidden.

2. Many experts suggest that creative problem analysis is critical to creative problem solving. To aid in this process, several approaches can be taken. Choose from the list below:

   • Identify a problem for discussion. Pose these two fundamental questions:

"What specifically is wrong?"

"What is not the problem?"

- Discuss what caused the problem in the first place, that is, where it started and where it came from. To get at the *root causes*, explore the chain of causes:

"Why do we have this problem? What caused it to occur?"

Which is caused by. . . .

Which is caused by. . . .

Which is caused by. . . .

- Do a *who, what, where, when, how* analysis. Discuss:

"Who is affected by the problem?"

"What actually happens?"

"Where does it happen? Where else could it occur, but it doesn't?"

"When does it happen? When does it not happen?"

"How does it happen?"

- Often, problems *repeat* themselves. Ask:

"Why does this problem reoccur?"

"Why do we keep getting sucked back into the situation?"

"What can we do to avoid the problem happening all over again?"

- Invite participants to use *metaphors* or develop *analogies* by completing the statement: "The problem is like [fill in the blank] in that or because it [complete the sentence]." Encourage everyone to let their minds roam freely during this exercise.

3. Use one or more of the following formats to explore any of the approaches above:

- Ask participants to write down their responses on index cards, then collect the cards or pass them around.
- Use a fishbowl or panel discussion format.
- Open the discussion using a call-on-the-next-speaker approach.
- Break into small groups for discussion, then ask participants to report their ideas out in the large group.

Challenging Assumptions

Overview

If you are conducting a problem-solving meeting, try challenging the status quo to help group members look at things from a new point of view and to obtain some interesting responses. One sure way to hear the same old answers is to ask the same questions, so encourage participants to take a truly deep look at the project or program from all angles for a fresh interpretation and fresh ideas.

Procedure

1. Have participants spend 5 minutes thinking about the project or program at hand. Ask them to ask themselves: "Does it have to be done the way it always has been?" Encourage them by saying, "Let's challenge our assumptions."

2. Ask participants to think about a tennis ball. It's round. It has a fuzzy covering applied in a certain design. Originally it was white. Now, it's often neon yellow or pink or orange. That's because someone asked: "Does it have to be white?"

3. Give another example: "Suppose the CEO of your company has ordered a design team to work on a new refrigerator for

the 21st Century." Ask participants to list the attributes of a conventional refrigerator.

These might be some of their observations:

- It is made of metal.
- It is a free-standing vertical cabinet with horizontal shelves.
- It is rectangular.
- It uses electricity.

After your participants consider and challenge these design "conventions," point out that an unconventional refrigerator might be placed under a counter and have vertical drawers to store items such as frozen pizza and frozen dinners. It might have a clear glass or plastic panel on the countertop so you could see and enjoy the colors of the fresh produce and fruit inside, and it could be powered by battery or nuclear fuel.

4. Suggest that the same method of challenging assumptions can be used with processes as well as products.

   For example, a local repertory theater does not have to host a black-tie ball to raise money. A school does not have to make mandated budget cuts "across the board." A business does not have to raise prices to increase profitability.

5. Now ask the group to think about its own "normal" ways of doing things. List the usual actions it might take, and then challenge the group to question what is sacred and raise new possibilities. Keep the climate exploratory—reminding participants that ideas can be rejected later.

Variation

If you're working with a large group, before the meeting talk with several people you think might be good leaders. Review your plan to start them challenging assumptions, and perhaps have them work on an example to make sure they understand the process. At the meeting, assign these leaders to groups of people, not to lead or direct the questions, but just to make sure the group stays on track.

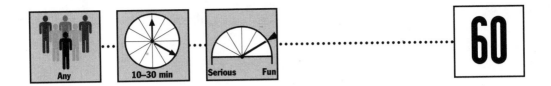
Inspired Cutouts*

Overview

Collages, those wonderful kaleidoscopic creations of bits and pieces of paper that form pictures or patterns, can provide real inspiration for problem solving. Your meeting participants can freshen their approach to a solution and be more creative by leafing through colorful magazines. When they see a certain picture, it may change the direction of their thoughts, help them so they see a different view, or even force a quick change of course.

Procedure

1. Take a large assortment of magazines with colorful pictures, scissors, paste or craft glue, and blank paper to the meeting.

2. Tell the participants they may search in the magazines for pieces to make a collage—an abstract composition made with fragments of paper.

3. They may, if they wish, actually cut up the magazines and paste together a collage, but they don't have to go that far.

*Based on a strategy developed by Bryan Mattimore.

Participants can form a mental collage by seeking out ideas and themes that are attractive to them. This exercise may help them see the problem they're working on in a slightly different light. At any rate, paging through a magazine frees the mind, as the person concentrates on something else.

For example, a group of architects might be frustrated by the necessity of fitting manufacturing equipment into a certain plan. As they let their minds wander through pages of pictures, building either mental or real collages, they're more likely to be receptive to a new idea, be willing to change a design, or see something in a pattern that sparks their imaginations.

A group of business strategists stumped in their attempt to move from a hierarchical system to a flatter organization might see a picture of a flock of geese that may help them visualize the company's proposed structure more easily.

At a meeting, a volunteer group was discussing how to recruit new volunteers and felt stuck. Looking at an image of wind surfers in a TV ad, someone said: "We're not making volunteering sound like it's fun or cool. Why don't we think of ways to promote volunteering by appealing to the fun people will have, rather than to the 'contribution' they would be making to society."

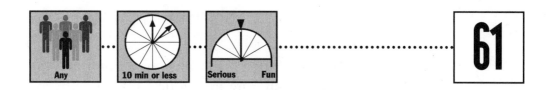

61

The Power of Two

....

Overview

This process is used both to promote creative problem solving and to reinforce the idea that two heads are indeed better than one.

Procedure

1. List a problem or issue in question form, like this:
   - *"How can we revitalize our program?"*
   - *"How can we improve our efficiency?"*
   - *"How can we reduce absenteeism?"*

2. Give an index card to each participant. Ask participants to answer the question you have chosen individually.

3. After all participants have completed their answers, arrange people into pairs and ask them to share their answers with one another.

4. Ask the pairs to create a *new* answer to the question, improving on each individual's response.

5. When all pairs have written new answers, compare the answers of each pair by sharing everyone's results with the others in the group.

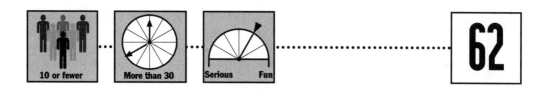

62

Mind Mapping

Overview

Mind mapping is a way to display your group's ideas in a non-linear format. It involves every participant in the creative problem-solving process. Asking participants to create a mind map during a meeting enables them to identify their ideas clearly and to use them to make creative suggestions to the entire group.

Procedure

1. Select the topic for mind mapping. Some possibilities include:

   • A problem or issue about which you want participants to create action ideas

   • A project to be planned by the participants

2. Construct a simple mind map using colors, images, or symbols.

   One example would be a trip to the grocery store during which a person shops from a mind map that categorizes items needed according to the departments in which they are found (for example, dairy, produce, and frozen foods).

Invite participants to cite simple examples from their daily lives of times when they could use mind mapping.

3. Provide paper, marking pens, and any other resources you think will help participants to create colorful, graphic mind maps. Give participants the mind-mapping assignment. Suggest that they begin their maps by creating a pictorial center, depicting the topic or main idea. Then encourage them to break the whole into smaller components and depict these components around the periphery of the map (using color and graphics). Urge them to represent each idea pictorially, using as few words as possible. Following this, they can fill in details as they come into their minds.

For example, imagine that your group is working on a proposal for requesting an additional staff member. A mind map might look like this:

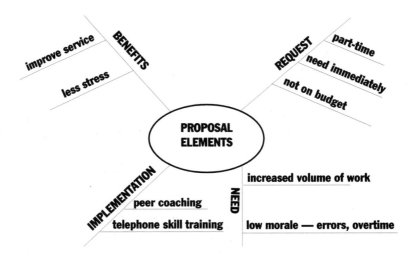

4. Provide plenty of time for participants to develop their mind maps. Encourage them to look at other people's work to stimulate ideas.

5. Ask participants to share their mind maps.

Variations

1. Assign a team mind map instead of having participants work individually.

2. Use computers to generate mind maps.

Managing Controversy and Conflict

No meeting worth its salt avoids controversy and conflict. They are normal, natural, and necessary in a group that is trying to accomplish important goals. In many meetings, however, controversy and conflict are not allowed to come to the surface. Even if they are, the group often becomes immobilized by the tension. When groups are able to confront controversy and conflict within their ranks and find win-win resolutions, they reach a stage of maturity that enables them to perform at very high levels.

This section features twelve strategies to manage controversy and conflict effectively. They are special processes you can use both when controversy and conflict are just starting to brew and when they are readily apparent. When you are helping a group cope with this type of tension, it is important to maintain a firm grip on the meeting. Sell the techniques you select as ways to move forward. Encourage participants to give them a chance to succeed. Progress may not be immediate, but tell the group that if it meets this challenge, it can accomplish anything.

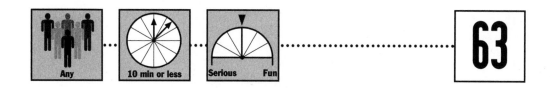

Any 10 min or less Serious Fun

63

Changing the Rules

Overview

The meeting is deteriorating into little squabbles, people are locking horns, and the discussion is going in circles. You need to do something dramatic to alter the climate of the meeting. Consider some of the ideas below.

Procedure

1. Tell participants that you have watched the meeting deteriorate in the last several minutes and you want to try something to see whether it will help them.

2. Explain that you would like to have everyone abide by a stringent ground rule for the next ten minutes. It is designed to change the way meeting participants are interacting with one another. Ask participants if they will agree to do it.

3. Select one or more of the following rule changes:

   • As each person speaks, he or she must first paraphrase what the previous speaker said. This ground rule will force participants to focus on views other than their own.

- Each speaker must "own" (take personal responsibility for) what he or she is saying. The speaker cannot speak for others and must insert "in my opinion" or "here's what I think" before speaking.

- Each participant will be given a quota of turns to speak. Give out a small quantity of objects (tickets, paper clips, coins, and so forth) to each participant. One item must be relinquished every time a turn is taken. When his or her supply is exhausted, the person can only listen.

- Only questions are allowed. Participants listen to what questions are on others' minds. No responses are given until every participant has had a chance to express a question.

- Participants must say what they *like* about another's idea before giving any criticism. Or they must use the phrase: "This could work *if.* . . ."

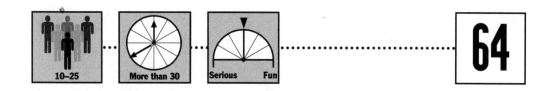

64

Active Debate

Overview

A debate can be a valuable method for promoting thinking and reflection, especially if participants are expected to take positions that are in opposition to one another. This design actively involves every participant, not just the debaters.

Procedure

1. Develop a statement that takes a position with regard to a controversial issue relating to your meeting topic.

   For example, an organization has decided to start an exterior beautification project for its international headquarters. The program is an exceptionally ambitious one, because the leaders believe image is important. The committee in charge must decide whether to turn the entire project over to an outside firm or to rely on the organization's building maintenance crew to do the job. Your statement could be: "We believe the maintenance crew is capable of great feats. Hiring just one additional landscaper and permitting limited overtime will allow the crew to do the job and save thousands for the company."

2. Divide the group into two debating teams. Assign (arbitrarily) the "pro" position to one team and the "con" position to the other.

3. Next, create two to four subgroups within each debating team. If, for example, twenty-four people are attending the meeting, you might create three "pro" subgroups and three "con" subgroups, each containing four members. Ask each subgroup to develop arguments for its assigned position. At the end of the discussion, have each subgroup select a spokesperson.

4. Set up two facing rows of two to four chairs each (depending on the number of subgroups created for each position) for the spokespersons of each team. Place the remaining participants behind their spokespersons. For the example above, the arrangement will look like this:

    ```
    XXX  X P        C X  XXX
    XXX  X R        O X  XXX
    XXX  X O        N X  XXX
    ```

    Begin the debate by having the spokespersons present their views. Refer to this process as "opening arguments."

5. After everyone has heard the opening arguments, stop the debate and reconvene the original subgroups. Ask the subgroups to strategize how to counter the opening arguments of the opposing side. Again, have each subgroup select a spokesperson, preferably a different person.

6. Resume the debate. Have the spokesperson give "counterarguments." As the debate continues (be sure to alternate between sides), encourage other participants to pass notes to their debaters with suggested arguments or rebuttals. Also, urge them to cheer or applaud the arguments of their debate-team representatives.

7. When you think it is appropriate, end the debate. Rather than declaring a winner, reconvene the entire group in a circle. Be sure to integrate the group by having participants sit next to people who were on opposing teams. Hold a full-group discussion on what participants learned about the issue from the debate experience. Also, ask participants to identify what they thought were the best arguments on both sides.

Variations

1. Add one or more empty chairs to the spokespersons' rows. Allow participants to occupy these empty chairs whenever they want to join the debate.

2. Start the activity immediately with the opening arguments of the debate. Proceed with a conventional debate, but frequently rotate the debaters.

3. If your time is limited, set aside a short time period to allow three people to speak in favor of the proposal under consideration and three people to speak against it.

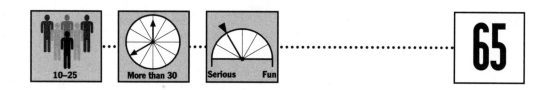

65

Removing Egos

Overview

This process is a discreet way to shrink oversized egos to standard group size. It is very effective at minimizing political debate. The process encourages participation from everyone, but tends to discourage any single participant from dominating the group.

Procedure

1. Explain to participants that you will be using a procedure that allows ideas to be evaluated without knowing who contributed them. Explain that this will be done to maximize group decision making and minimize individual politicking.

2. Follow these steps.

   • State the task clearly and succinctly.

   For example, a future planning task force is charged with developing ideas for new goals and initiatives over the next five years.

   • Give everyone index cards and ask participants to write their ideas on their index cards *in silence*. They may write as many ideas as they like (one idea per card).

- Collect the cards. Reshuffle them and distribute them to a card reader. Do not allow discussion at this point! Have the reader read each card aloud while someone writes the idea it contains on a flip chart. Assign a number to each suggestion. (Ask participants not to reveal who presented a specific idea.) Promote the notion that all the ideas are now the "property of the group."

- Now allow the individuals who wrote them to discuss all the ideas listed, clarifying or condensing them. Discourage outright lobbying for an idea.

- Give a new index card to each person. Have each participant write "First Vote" in a corner of the card and have him or her rank the top five ideas from the flip chart, giving a score of "5" to the top-ranked idea, "4" to the next ranked, and so forth. Collect the cards. Total the scores for each idea and arrange the ideas in the order of their scores—highest to lowest—on the flip chart.

- Have the group debate the items on the list a second time.

- Have the meeting participants label fresh cards "Second Vote" and write on them three to five of the ideas they favor *without consulting with the others in the group.*

- Collect and tally the final rankings and clarify each one for the participants so that everyone understands the final decisions.

Variation

Ask participants: "What would be the ideal course of action we could take to satisfy all of the viewpoints in our group?" Focusing on this question may also be a way to minimize ego involvement.

66

Breaking a Stalemate[*]

Overview

When a conflict completely overtakes a group and neither side will budge, try to move things along by asking everyone to agree to engage in a four-step process during which each party prepares a presentation about the other's position.

Procedure

1. Tell the group that, in your opinion, the conflict has deteriorated into an argument about who's right and who's wrong, rather than a discussion of the actual issues. Explain that you have a process that may help to break the stalemate.

2. Ask each side to prepare a four-part presentation:

---

*Based on a strategy developed by Bob Guns.

The Conflict We're Having

Discuss and agree on the opposing positions being taken. Be objective and descriptive about the other group's position, and show that you have listened well to your opponents. Don't disparage their position. Be respectful about it.

> *For example, consider a conflict between the academic dean of a college and the faculty members on grade inflation. The faculty might state: "It seems that we have opposite views about grade inflation. You want a greater distribution of grades so that we appear to have higher standards than what is reflected in the current grade distribution. We think that the higher grades reflect well on us as a faculty. We must be doing something right."*

What Concerns Us

Share your own feelings, concerns, and needs about the issue.

> *The faculty might further say: "We are concerned that students will become obsessed with how they are graded, rather than with how they can be effective learners. We also worry that focusing on grade inflation emphasizes making things tougher for students—not rethinking what our basic teaching goals are and what we can do to facilitate them."*

What We'd Like to Suggest

Share a creative suggestion you have to get beyond where the group is stuck.

> *The faculty might then say: "What would be ideal is to agree to be more explicit about the performance criteria for different grading outcomes. If most students do well, there's no reason to have a grading curve."*

What We're Willing to Do About It

Make a statement about the actions your side is prepared to make to create a better situation.

The faculty then might conclude: "We'd be willing to submit to the academic dean our current grading criteria and obtain his recommendations on how they can be made clearer."

---

3. Invite each side to make its presentation.
4. Ask each side to comment on the other's presentation.
   - *"How much did the other side understand about your position?"*
   - *"What suggestions from them hold promise?"*
   - *"Is there a basis for moving to a win-win resolution of the problem?"*

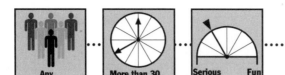

67

Collaboration in Conflict Resolution

Overview

Sometimes, an issue is so explosive or the meeting is so tense that a full-group discussion of a conflict seems unproductive. The best approach may be to adopt a small-group approach that minimizes open conflict and maximizes collaboration.

Procedure

1. Devise three questions to ask participants about the conflict affecting the group. Here are three possibilities:

   - *"How important is it that we resolve this conflict?"*
   - *"What is the ideal resolution to this conflict?"*
   - *"What practical ideas do you have to resolve this conflict?"*

   Express the questions in a way that invites concrete answers. Avoid highly open-ended questions.

2. Inform participants that you would like the group to try a collaborative approach to conflict resolution that avoids extended discussion or public fighting. This approach would work well in a situation such as this:

About 60 percent of the workers at a California branch of a national manufacturing company are of Hispanic background, and the branch has a team of managers that is 50 percent Hispanic and 50 percent non-Hispanic. The workers want all company communications to be presented in a bilingual format. The Hispanic managers support the request, but the non-Hispanic managers are opposed to it, citing cost and lack of precedence at other branches.

3. Divide participants into trios. Give each member of the trio one of the three conflict assessment questions you have created and a paper and pencil. Ask each trio member to interview the other participants and obtain (and record) the answers to his or her assigned question.

4. Form three subgroups, one each for all the participants who have been assigned each of the questions. For example, if there are eighteen participants, arranged in trios, six of them will have been assigned the same question.

5. Ask each subgroup to pool its data and summarize it. Then ask each subgroup to report to the entire group what they have learned about the group's response to the question assigned to it.

6. Ask the group to reflect on what the data that has emerged means, assess the situation, and decide what to do next.

Variation

Invite the participants to devise their own questions. Using the questions they have devised, pair up participants and have them interview one another. Poll the full group afterward to obtain the results. (This variation is appropriate when dealing with a large group.)

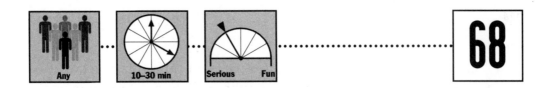

Differences of Opinion

Overview

When differences of opinion emerge in a group over time, the comments exchanged become argumentative rather than constructive. Arguments frequently lead nowhere and can polarize the participants in a very destructive way. The process described here enables a group to review its differences of opinion in a positive manner.

Procedure

1. Create a list of issues on which there have been disagreements within the group.

   Take, for example, a search committee that has battled over the suitability of different applicants for the position it is trying to fill. Their differences of opinion might include the following:

   - *The value of resumes*
   - *The reliability of letters of recommendations*
   - *The profile of an ideal candidate*

2. List the various areas of disagreement on a flip chart. Check with the group to make sure that you have listed them accurately and add anything you may have missed.

3. Choose any voting procedure that enables the group to select the top three or four concerns.

4. Form the participants into three or four subgroups, one for each concern the group has chosen. Ask each subgroup to discuss one of the topics on which there is a difference of opinion. Invite the subgroups to recommend ways the full group can resolve or manage the disagreement.

5. Ask each subgroup to summarize its discussion for the entire group. Obtain reactions from the total group.

Variation

Rather than end the activity with subgroup reports, create a panel or fishbowl discussion of the issue.

Active Self-Assessment

Overview

This exercise allows the participants to share their attitudes with others about a topic of importance to the group. It permits the facilitator to gauge both the feelings and beliefs of the participants, and it also serves as a springboard for group discussion.

Procedure

1. Create a list of statements to be read to participants that will assess their attitudes and feelings about a given subject. Here are some examples:

   I believe we should go forward with the waste disposal project.

   Parents have the primary responsibility for their children's behavior.

   I feel comfortable with our current policy on conflict of interest.

2. Ask the participants to stand in the back of the room and clear the chairs or desks to one side.

3. Create a rating scale of numbers 1 through 5 in the front of the room by posting numbers on the wall.

4. Explain that statements will be read one at a time. After hearing each statement, each participant should stand in front of the rating number that best matches his or her feelings on the subject. Number "1" could be "Strongly Agree" with the range extending to "5" for "Strongly Disagree."

5. As each statement is read, participants should move to the places in the room that best match their opinions. After lines form in front of the various positions, invite some participants to explain why they have chosen their positions.

6. After hearing the opinions of others, invite anyone who wishes to alter his or her position on the scale to do so.

7. Continue reading the individual statements, requesting participants to move to the numbers that best match their opinions.

8. Break participants into subgroups according to position chosen. Give them written copies of the statements and ask them to discuss them among themselves.

9. Now, ask participants to consider their stand on each item privately. Have them assign a number to each statement that reflects their *final* level of agreement or disagreement.

Variations

1. In a larger setting, have the participants first choose a response to the statements and then move to the numbered posts.

2. Begin with small-group discussion and then proceed with individual (private) assessment.

70

Hot Issues*

Overview

This process allows members of a committee or board to look at the project they're working on from different perspectives: those of participants themselves as well as those of others who have a stake in the outcome. This helps the group to overcome any short-sighted view that does not take the larger system into consideration. It is an especially good technique to use to cool down hot issues.

Procedure

1. Take to the meeting the following materials:
    *   Flip-chart paper
    *   Tape
    *   Post-it® Notes
    *   3" x 5" cards in three different colors
    *   A large supply of envelopes
    *   A stopwatch
    *   A whistle

*Based on a strategy developed by Bill Matthews.

2. Determine the controversial problem the group needs to solve.

   For example, in the case of a committee formed to purchase land for a new city football stadium, the group is caught between the personalities of two separate leaders: the mayor and the head of a community organization that raises large sums of money. The mayor wants to buy a former landfill property, and the community leader wants to purchase a prime site close to throughways. Some members fear the committee may be overlooking other land-purchasing opportunities.

3. Limit the scope of the issues; describe the problem as succinctly as possible in one or two sentences for the group.

   For the case above, the statement might read: "The committee must decide on a site for the new sports stadium by April 30. Two sites are under consideration. The group needs to decide whether other sites should also be considered and, if so, which ones."

4. Brainstorm and list the perspectives of all the people who have a stake in the outcome.

   In the example, stakeholders would include spectators, investors, sports organizations, the city, the community, concessionaires, suppliers, and others with special interests in the project.

5. Write each possible perspective at the top of a flip-chart page as though it were a title, one to each page, and divide each page into three columns labeled F, A, and Q.

6. Hang pages at intervals around the room.

7. Give each person a supply of Post-it® Notes and a pen and explain these ground rules:

   • Every person must contribute to every chart.

   • Each person must list anything he or she knows to be *true* as a *fact* on a separate note and place it in the column marked "F" on any appropriate sheet. All these notes should be also be labeled "F."

- Each person must list what he or she believes to be an *assumption* on a separate note and place it in the "A" column on the appropriate sheets. These notes must be labeled "A."

- Each person then must list information he or she needs to know on separate notes labeled "Q" for *question* and stick the notes to the appropriate sheets in the "Q" column.

8. Set a time limit for the process—probably 20 to 30 minutes is sufficient. Divide the group members into three subgroups and assign the subgroups to different charts, where they will write their notes and post them.

9. Have the subgroups rotate in one direction after they finish one flip-chart page, moving to each in turn until they have finished posting their facts, assumptions, and questions.

10. Watch to make sure that everyone follows instructions. Keep them informed about the time remaining.

11. Blow the whistle when time is up, but allow the participants a little extra time if they need it.

12. As a group, talk through the differing views, challenging facts and assumptions and asking for data to support statements.

13. Create a plan to gather information in order to answer questions that were posted.

14. Look for relationships among the perspectives. Also check to see whether there are actually separate aspects to any one view.

15. Ask the group members whether they are looking at the issue in a way that is blocking the group's ability to act.

16. Next, have the group sort the data and create a plan of action to solve the problem. This can be done in various ways, but here is a good method.

    Write the name of each of the stakeholder groups identified in Step 5 on a separate envelope. Provide a stack of 3" x 5" cards (in three different colors) to each participant and then give one of the envelopes to each person. Have participants check the names on the envelopes they received. Tell them to write an appropriate fact, assumption, or question on a card, using the color you have designated for each category, and place it into the envelope.

    Have participants pass the envelopes along and repeat the procedure until everyone has contributed at least one card to every envelope.

    Now envelopes can be given to the appropriate stakeholders for discussion in the group from different points of view.

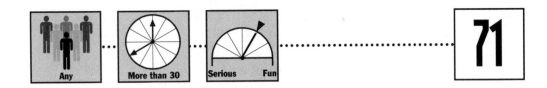
Arguing the Flip Side

Overview

One effective way to defuse a meeting that has erupted into a conflict so severe that it is blocking action is to have the participants reverse roles. People may have boxed themselves into all-or-nothing thinking patterns and may not know how to escape from that trap. If they concentrate on presenting one another's viewpoints, it is possible the participants can resolve misunderstandings, gain more realistic perceptions, and reach a clearer understanding of one another's positions.

Procedure

1. Identify an issue on which participants have boxed themselves into all-or-nothing thinking patterns.

   Consider, for example, that you are facilitating a medical association meeting. The association is composed of both physicians and nurses on a hospital staff, who are at odds with the hospital administration because of proposed severe cost-cutting measures; however, the doctors and nurses also completely disagree with one another over exactly how much the measures will affect patient care. You will want to have the doctors look at the nurses' side of the argument and the nurses consider the doctors' point of view.

2. Encourage the group to be willing to experience role reversal, a time-honored conflict-resolution technique. Explain that you will ask the group to spend from 10 to 20 minutes discussing the dispute that has arisen. During that time, participants will be asked to take on the role of someone with a different position from their own. If only two sides have been presented, participants merely switch their positions for a short time. If there are more than two points of view, ask participants to adopt any position other than their own.

3. Facilitate the role-reversal discussion. Keep encouraging participants to stay in role. Although there may be some laughter during this process, try to keep the mood serious.

4. After the time is up, ask participants the following questions:

   • *"Did you feel that your own views were accurately stated by others adopting your position?"*

   • *"What insights did you obtain from arguing the flip side of the issue?"*

5. Continue a normal discussion of the conflict to determine whether the role-reversal process has helped to move the group beyond where they were.

Variations

1. Pair up participants with opposite views and ask them to argue the flip side with each other. This may be less awkward than conducting a whole-group discussion.

2. If the group is fairly small and the members know one another relatively well, it's fun to switch identities instead of just switching positions. Simply have the participants move their name tents and pretend to be the other person while presenting the other person's position.

3. As an alternative to this role-reversal exercise, list competing ideas as a group. Ask participants to state the advantages of ideas that differ from their own. Publicly stating the good points of an opponent's solution may reduce the tension in a polarized group.

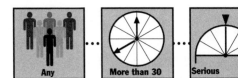

72

Perception Checking

Overview

One way to end a stalemate is to shine the light of reality on it. This method of managing conflict carries role reversal one step further. Often, conflict worsens because people misunderstand their opponents' positions. This exercise allows a person holding one view to state what he or she believes is the opponent's position. Then the other person has a chance to do the same. The exercise is sure to be an eyeopener for both sides, showing perceptions a bit removed from reality. It may even lead to a new spirit of compromise.

Procedure

1. Divide the meeting participants into subgroups according to the position they have taken in the controversy.

   For example, suppose it has been suggested that a governing board of supervisors be expanded from three to five members. Those who want to continue with three board members fear loss of control, and even a takeover, if two new members are added. They irrationally believe that the new members will align themselves with a supervisor considered to be "a loose cannon." Those who favor a five-member board claim it will lighten the workload for the present board, allow the board to move more quickly, and add new dimensions to an understanding of difficult issues.

2. Ask each group to prepare a report showing its understanding of the opponent's views. This report may contain some assumptions that might not have been clearly expressed, as well as a recap of things that have been said. The report should then be presented to the total group.

3. Allow the opposing group to react to the report, either immediately or by preparing a more formal response.

4. After the opposing group has provided feedback about the report, allow this group to make its own presentation. Then ask for feedback from the other side, just as before.

5. With some of the conflict eradicated, or at least broken down into negotiable chunks, you may now conduct a discussion of the issues and hear ways to solve the problems based on information gathered during both presentations and the feedback sessions.

Variations

1. This same technique will be effective even if there are more than two sides involved in the conflict. Simply follow the same procedure, allowing each group to present its report and then asking for feedback from the other groups.

2. Shorten the entire process by keeping the full group together and inviting individuals to summarize the points of view of others who are in conflict with their own views. Urge participants to follow these rules:

   • State not just what has been said, but the feelings and concerns you imagine are behind it.

   • Stay objective; avoid sarcasm or disparagement.

   • Give others the right to respond to the accuracy of the summary.

10–25   More than 30   Serious   Fun

73

Fishbowl Meeting[*]

Overview

Asking the participants at your meeting to use a fishbowl design is an excellent way to help them resolve a controversy without undue antagonism. This technique forces the proponents of different sides of an issue both to give and to receive advice. It should be a growth experience for all involved and help the two sides to work together toward a solution.

Procedure

1. Before the participants arrive, set up a tight circle of chairs, with a second circle directly outside the first. Both circles together should contain enough chairs to accommodate the number of participants you are expecting.

2. Provide a brief introduction that outlines the status of the dispute between the opposing sides.

   Consider, for example, a joint meeting of the editorial staff of a monthly magazine and members of the publication's production

---

*Based on a strategy developed by Rod Napier and Matti Gershenfeld.

department. The two entities have been natural enemies for years over subjects such as work distribution and deadlines; however, the magazine has a new publisher who has little patience with the arguments presented by either group. He wants the schedule to be workable and realistic for both departments. He means business and has asked you to facilitate the meeting to produce a new schedule.

3. Divide the group *randomly* into two subgroups.

4. Tell the first group to takes seats in the inner circle of chairs. Direct the second group to sit in the outer circle behind the others.

5. Ask those in the inner circle, Group A, to discuss one issue, such as why deadlines are not being met. Direct those seated in the outer circle only to listen and observe and *not* to take part in the discussion. Allow 6 to 10 minutes for the discussion.

6. At the end of the time limit, ask the two groups to trade seats. Now Group B is in the inner circle and will have the same length of time to discuss the issue while Group A members listen and observe. Although the goal is for each group to come up with independent solutions, Group B may borrow ideas they hear and build on them during their time in the inner circle of the fishbowl.

7. Have Groups A and B trade places as many times as necessary to reach a solution or complete a plan of action, but always allow equal time to each group.

Variation

Keep participants with the same views in the same group. It will be interesting to see how they express themselves without any opposition.

Going Beyond the Pros and Cons

A popular way to analyze any proposal beyond simply listing pros and cons is to use a SWOT* analysis. Such an analysis focuses on four ways to evaluate the proposal: Strengths, Weaknesses, Opportunities, and Threats. Strengths and weaknesses pertain to the *internal* resources your organization or group has. Opportunities and threats apply to issues *external* to the proposal or strategy.

Procedure

1. Explain what SWOT means. Find out who is familiar with the tool. Indicate that SWOT is a structured, step-by-step way to look at any proposal or strategy.

2. Begin with a discussion of the *strengths* your group or organization brings to the proposal or strategy under review. Look at such things as:

   • Expertise

   • Motivation

*From J. William Pfeiffer, Leonard D. Goodstein, and Timothy M. Nolan, *Shaping Strategic Planning: Frogs, Dragons, Bees, and Turkey Tails.* Scott, Foresman and Company and Jossey-Bass/Pfeiffer, 1989.

- Financial resources
- Physical resources and facilities
- Reputation
- Strategic direction
- Efficiency

3. Continue with a discussion of the *weaknesses* that your group or organization brings to the proposal or strategy under review. Point out that *weaknesses can be overcome.*

4. Next, discuss the *opportunities* before you, that is, the favorable conditions that exist outside of your group or organization that you can take advantage of, such as market conditions.

5. Finally, discuss the *threats,* the external obstacles facing you, beyond the ones you have direct control over. These represent the hurdles confronting you that you must cope with, even if you cannot completely overcome them.

6. Having explored a proposal or strategy from these vantage points, encourage the group to come to conclusions about the proposal or strategy at hand.

Building Consensus
and Commitment

Con | sen | sus
& |
Com | mit | ment

It's now crunch time. Your group has been exploring ideas and debating its options. Some ideas will have to be discarded—for now, at least. Difficult decisions need to be reached, and priorities need to be established. Agreement and commitment are the order of the day.

Most experts agree that groups should make important decisions by building consensus, as opposed to voting. A consensus exists when everyone is willing to support and commit to a specific decision. It may not be everyone's first choice, but everyone can live with the decision being reached. When a group builds a consensus, there is greater commitment to implement the group's decision. With voting, a disgruntled minority usually lags in their commitment to the implementation phase.

This section contains twelve strategies to build consensus and commitment. The first to be presented are techniques to narrow down the options a group has generated. Next come ways to obtain a consensus that feels inclusive. Finally, you will find strategies to inspire commitment to the decisions that have been made.

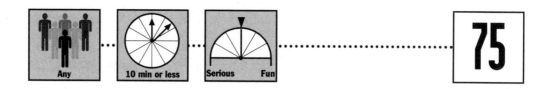
Billboard Ranking

Overview

Often the ideas presented as a group nears consensus are neither right nor wrong. As the group attempts to reach a decision that needs to be made, it has to consider also the values, opinions, ideas, and preferences of the people involved. This activity will help stimulate a final round of reflection and discussion.

Procedure

1. Identify an issue on which different suggestions have been circulating in the group. As an example, consider this problem:

   The president of a string of art gallery/stores operating in good downtown locations in small cities in the Northeast wants to add a new layer to the business. The gallery/stores are well known for lower-end (but quality) artwork and picture frames that sell for under $100. The business has been extremely successful, and the president now wants to add higher-end products to sell for $500 and up. The store managers are fiercely divided on the plan. Half are reluctantly willing to try adding the line, but about the same number do not believe their customers will pay that price. They suggest, instead, opening a pilot store under a new name. The managers all *have large financial interests in their individual stores, so the ultimate decision will be theirs.*

2. List and number the ideas that have been discussed so far.

    For example, considering the problem above, the managers have considered three options:

    - *Investigate the costs of setting up a new store;*
    - *Test the more expensive artwork at three of the existing thirty stores for six months;*
    - *Continue to operate the thirty stores just as they have been operated for the past five years.*

3. Give each participant a pad of Post-it® Notes. Ask the subgroups to write the number of each item on the list on a separate sheet.

4. Ask the subgroups to sort the sheets so that the number corresponding to the action they most prefer is on top, and the remaining items are placed consecutively in rank order.

5. Create a "billboard" on which participants can display their preferences. (The notes also can be attached to a flip chart or a large sheet of paper taped to a wall.)

6. Compare and contrast the rankings that are now visually displayed. The display may indicate that consensus has already been reached. If it does not, at least it will show where more work is needed.

Variation

If the group is large, divide participants into subgroups and ask each subgroup to come to an agreement on how to rank the options. Then do the procedure above with the subgroups.

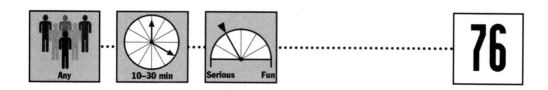

76

Multivoting

Overview

Multivoting is an efficient and effective way to narrow the choices from a long list of decision options. Once the list has been narrowed, it is often easier to obtain consensus. The members of the group prepare a list of possible solutions to a complex problem and are permitted to narrow the list themselves by casting a specified number of votes until only a few possibilities, those acceptable to the majority of the voters, remain. This eliminates the loss of many good ideas, one of the problems created by a single vote on a long list of items. This technique is more likely to keep those second-tier ideas viable.

Procedure

1. List on a flip chart all possible alternatives that could solve the particular problem, along with their attendant difficulties and advantages. If two or more alternatives are very similar, combine them, as long as the group agrees they should be combined. Consider this situation as an example:

A small independent award-winning film company (owned by its two hundred employees) is planning to make a high-adventure film. The company is based on the East Coast, but the movie plot requires ocean, mountain, and desert scenes. The company has a large number of locations it can travel to for filming, but each has some kind of major or minor problem associated with it, such as high cost, tax implications, or poor schools for employees' children, as well as some major advantages. Time is running out and a decision on where to film must be made in a matter of weeks.

2. Tell the participants to think carefully about what options they can accept.

3. Pass out ballots and ask the participants to vote for each alternative they find acceptable. They may vote for as many as they want. Inform them, however, that only alternatives receiving half of all the possible votes will remain in contention and then placed on a second ballot.

4. Count the ballots and hold a discussion of the remaining choices. Then vote again. Keep the alternatives that receive half of all the possible votes on the second ballot on the list.

5. Determine at this point whether more voting is needed to narrow the choices to begin working on a consensus.

Variation

If you do not have the time to follow the above method, have all the members write down those options they like best. Let them select up to one-third of the items on the list. For example, if there are fifteen items on the list, a participant may select up to five. Members can vote by a show of hands or, if there is a need for secrecy, on paper ballots. To use this procedure:

- Count the hands or collect the ballots and reduce the list by removing those options that received very few votes. (This will, of course, depend on the size of the group. For a small group, one or two votes may be the determining factor for removal. If the group has fifteen or more members, perhaps four or five votes would make a good cutoff number.)

- Repeat these steps as often as necessary to reduce the remaining items on the list. Continue until only a few items remain.

- At this point, if no clear favorite is apparent, have the group discuss which is the best choice.

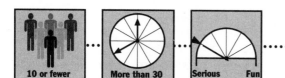
Weighing the Options

Overview

This is an excellent follow-up to multivoting. When many solutions to a problem have been suggested, probably the most efficient way to select the best ones is to have the group weigh them *against specific standards*. The process can be as simple or as comprehensive as necessary in order to achieve consensus. It can be used by small groups as well as large ones.

Procedure

1. On a large flip chart, prepare a list of all the remaining solutions to the problem on which the group is focusing. Consider this example:

   Radio Station KCHD plays primarily soft rock music and has been highly successful over the years; however, the station's advertising sales staff has approached three new commercial sponsors who, combined, would be purchasing about 35 percent of the station's air time. The board of directors is pleased with the potential business, but the sponsors say they think their products will do better with the country music set and point to its growing popularity in the region. They want the station to play half country music and half soft rock. Some members of the board of directors want nothing to do with anything new; some are willing to try a small percentage of country music; a few are willing to try 50 percent; and others favor shades in-between. Some fear the station will lose listeners as well as other advertisers; others fear the station will miss the boat if it doesn't adapt to its sponsors' wishes.

2. Before going any further, propose a set of standards against which the group can evaluate its options.

   In the example above, the standards might be:
   - *Enhances the station's image*
   - *Attracts new listeners and advertisers*
   - *Retains current listeners and advertisers*
   - *Provides a fall-back position*

3. Ask the participants to discuss each option according to the standards you have suggested. Be sure to go through each option, collecting judgments. Don't allow the process to become bogged down in a campaign for a particular option.

4. Invite each participant to rate each option in terms of how well it meets the standards being examined. Use a 1 through 5 scale, with a "1" suggesting a weak evaluation and a "5" suggesting a strong evaluation. Record the scores, and then rank the items according to the total score for each. If you feel some standards loom larger in importance than others, you may want to suggest multiplying them by relative weights.

5. Have the group examine the results and try to reach consensus.

Variation

Ask the group to brainstorm its own standards for judging the choices available.

Small Group to Large Group Consensus

Overview

This strategy builds consensus from the ground up. It is often easier to achieve consensus through discussion in small groups. Although for use with any size group, this is a particularly effective way to help a large group make a decision.

Procedure

1. Review the issue under discussion and identify some of the views expressed or options considered.

2. Ask the participants whether they agree with your review.

   For example, consider this situation: A cardboard box manufacturer is one of the few nonunionized companies in the industry, but it has been experiencing some internal problems recently because of some heavy-handed, inflexible management. Department managers fear the workers will unionize. One set of managers wants to establish an internal arbitration system to provide workers relief from poor practices and diffuse any movement toward unionizing. The opposing managers fear an internal system will clear the way for a union takeover.

3. Divide the participants into smaller groups (the size depends on the total number of meeting participants). Ask each of the smaller groups to develop a proposal to be presented to the entire group. Set a time limit on the discussion.

4. Ask each small group to select a member to present its proposal to the large group. As they do this, record the possible solutions on a flip chart.

5. Ask the large group to discuss the possibilities presented by the smaller groups. As facilitator, you should look for and later note for the group the points in common among the presentations. Then call for a consensus decision on these points. Also, take care to identify areas of disagreement.

6. Now have the small groups work on the contested points and try to draw up new proposals to resolve them. Again, set a definite time limit and make the group meet it. It will help them accomplish more in less time.

7. Have someone from each group present the new proposals and, just as you did before, try to find a consensus. It may be necessary to repeat these steps several times until the entire group is able to reach a consensus.

Variation

Another way to speed up consensus for a large group is to pass out index cards to each person. Ask the people to write down on the cards five good ideas that have been expressed. Also ask them how close they feel to reaching consensus and ask them to indicate their opinions on how close the group is to a consensus. They can use the scale described in "Polling for Consensus," the next strategy in this book.

List the ideas from the cards on a flip chart and discuss them. Then ask the group to narrow the list down to three ideas. Review those ideas and check carefully to see whether a consensus can be reached. If not, ask the participants to narrow the three ideas to two, and then to decide between them.

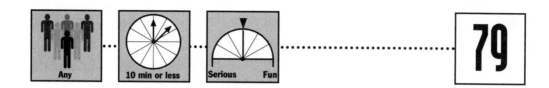
Polling for Consensus [*]

Overview

Polling for consensus is one good way to take the pulse of a group. When you survey a group, you are better able to pinpoint the degrees of difference among the participants' opposition or support of an idea and to assess how close the sides really are. Your polling results will tell you whether further discussion is needed or whether the opposing groups are ready at this point to seek a serious solution.

Procedure

1. Tell the participants that they have reached a point at which no new ideas are being presented and that they are merely recycling the same opinions and positions. Explain that this is the time to conduct a poll to see whether a decision is near.

   As an example, consider this scenario: The top managers of a toy manufacturing company are concerned because they are losing market share. The company's method has always been for engineers

---

*Based on a strategy developed by Dee Kelsey and Pam Plumb.

to design the toys and, after prototypes are produced, to turn a roomful of children loose to play with the new products. This has worked well for the company in the past. Some people have proposed a similar but separate experiment to allow adults to test the toys, too. Their reasoning is that adults are the ones who actually purchase the toys.

2. Restate the plan under consideration. Explain to the group that there are a number of different stages of readiness for consensus. Participants can feel any one of several ways in response to a proposed plan, as follows:

   A. Willing to accept the plan

   B. Admitting that the plan is a fair solution, but not one that he or she can get really excited about

   C. Not fully agreeing with the plan and feeling the need to explain why it is not acceptable, but not willing to try to block the idea

   D. Disagreeing with the decision and feeling strongly enough about it to try to exercise all of his or her influence to stop the plan

   F. Expressing concern that the group is not able to agree on the plan and wanting to do more work on the concept before reaching consensus

3. List the different possibilities on the flip chart by letter. Ask the participants to indicate where they stand on the readiness scale for this particular issue. They may indicate this by raising their hands as you call out the letters or they may want to jot down the letter on an index card to be collected and tallied.

4. The results will show you whether more work needs to be done. If there are a lot of A's and B's, then you and the group may determine that consensus has been reached. If the

grades are mostly C's and D's, and if there are some F's, more discussion time is needed.

5. No matter what the results of the poll, it's smart to ask whether participants have any comments to make. Even when only one person disagrees with the decision, it's important to listen to that person's position.

Variation

There are times when more than one option remains under discussion. Another way to bring the group closer to consensus is to conduct straw polls on the remaining two or three options. If you choose this method, make sure you tell the participants this is not a binding vote but merely an attempt to assess positions at the moment to obtain "a sense of the meeting."

Hearing from the Minority

Overview

When a group is attempting to build consensus, it is important to provide some kind of forum for the minority to speak, as well as to collect any splinter ideas they might have that could be extremely important to the project. Providing a way for the minority to be heard is a practical way to tidy up loose ends, and it can be a healing one as well in terms of the group's future ability to work together.

Procedure

1. As a group is discussing a course of action, ask: "Who is still concerned about this proposal? What problems do you have with it?" Set aside time for the "minority" to speak.

2. Another possibility is to provide time for the group that is obviously in the minority to make a statement. You might set aside 15 or 30 minutes at a meeting when consensus seems near.

3. Ask the dissenters to conduct a panel discussion about their position and answer questions from the majority members.

Make it clear you want them to discuss their ideas in detail because they might have some very good thoughts, lost or submerged in the arguments, that could be used in the final project. Even if that does not happen, at least they will have been heard.

4. Another option is to ask those who are in the minority to come to the next meeting with a counterproposal to the one that seems to be supported by most of the participants.

   Consider this real-life example: A religious organization applied to a municipality for permission to build a group home for adolescent girls who had come from homes where they were abused. The organization wanted to buy one of a series of mansions that lined the main street of the town. The night the plan was introduced before the town council a small, but outspoken group of neighbors, who had heard rumors about the plan, fought the idea feverishly. The neighbors complained that the organization wouldn't have the funds to keep up the property. They said the girls were bad and might be thieves, would surely be a bad influence on younger children and boys of their own age, might party all night, and subsequently would destroy the neighborhood. They refused to listen to the religious organization's plans and even booed its representative. It was apparent to someone in the crowd that the meeting was going nowhere and would not if this continued. He suggested the town council select three people from the minority group and have them meet with the religious organization to iron out some of the problems. Given a little time to cool down, the two groups met, a deal was struck, the organization got its group home, and the neighbors received the safeguards they wanted.

5. After hearing from the minority, ask the total group whether anyone has suggestions for alleviating the concerns expressed.

Variation

In any group, people who are concerned about the direction being taken may not speak up. Consider polling each participant to determine whether reservations exist.

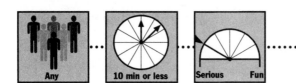

Super-Majority Voting[*]

Overview

Building consensus in a group can be very time-consuming. To avoid the temptation of settling matters by simple majority voting, it might be feasible to set a super-majority standard, such as 75 percent agreement. If this standard is set in advance, then it is likely that a climate of consensus building will be created—even though 100 percent agreement is not being sought. Super majorities indicate that there is a sizable agreement and willingness to implement what has been decided. The greater a role participants have in the process of creating a super majority, the more likely they are to make it work. Here is one such process.

Procedure

1. Point out that important decisions require sizable support. Note that the U.S. Constitution cannot be amended unless 75 percent of the states approve. Also, a presidential veto cannot be overthrown unless two-thirds of Congress votes to override it. A president cannot be removed from office after an

---

*Based on a strategy developed by Mary Margaret Palmer.

impeachment vote in the House without a two-thirds majority in the Senate.

2. Make sure participants agree to the percentage of votes needed prior to a final discussion of a proposed course of action.

3. Draw a 0 to 5 scale on newsprint. Ask participants to define in their own words what each point on the scale might signify. For example, they might decide that a "5" indicates that the proposed decision is something "to die for," whereas a "0" might signify that the proposed decision is something one is "dead set against."

4. Next, have the group create a decision standard, such as the following: "Seventy-five percent of the participants must rate the proposed decision as a 5, and none of the remaining votes can be below a 3."

5. Rate the proposed course of action on the scale to see whether the standard has been met. If not, discuss how the proposal can be modified to be more acceptable.

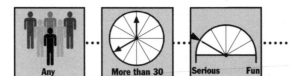

Comparing the Remaining Options

Overview

When participants have championed a course of action at a meeting, they tend to round up political support. In the push to gain agreement, participants may not give other available options the careful scrutiny they deserve. A process during which alternative ideas are weighed systematically is a welcome remedy.

Procedure

1. Point out that the group has developed more than two possible options. Explain that, at this point, a wide-open discussion of alternative courses of action might lead to a lot of politicking on the part of individual group members. As one proposal is pushed, those who agree with it may do what they can to corral support. Propose, instead, a careful, highly structured analysis of each course of action.

2. Identify up to five courses of action that have emerged so far after lengthy discussion.

3. Ask the group to discuss each course of action against *each of the others*. This means that Proposal A will be compared to

Proposal B, C, and so forth. Then, Proposal B will be compared to A, C, and so forth, one at a time. This process will continue until each of the proposals has been compared to the others.

4. After the multiple comparison process has been completed, determine the relative strength of each proposal.

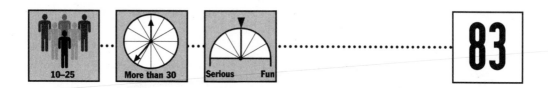

Putting a Decision "On Trial"

Overview

Because so much may be at stake, a consensus often takes a long time to attain. Here is a process that may work for you when your group is facing a momentous decision and cannot afford to become gridlocked.

Procedure

1. State the problem and provide an objective review of the discussions that have been held until now.

2. Suggest that any decision reached today is "on trial" for two months (or suggest any other time frame you feel is appropriate). After the trial period is over, the decision will be opened for review. Obtain agreement on this process.

3. Help the group to arrive at a decision by consensus or by a super-majority vote.

4. When a decision has been made, invite participants to brainstorm ways in which the decision can be evaluated after it is implemented. List the ideas for all to see.

5. Randomly create small groups and give each group 15 minutes to react to the list and either choose its two best ideas or develop one or two new ideas that build on the brainstormed list. Ask each small group to select someone to present its ideas.

6. Reconvene the total group and ask each subgroup presenter to report his or her group's two recommendations.

7. As a group, decide whether to accept all the ideas or to negotiate the best ones.

84

Moving Toward Consensus

Overview

Consensus building may be hampered by the dynamics of large group discussion. In this design, a group discovers whether there is an emerging consensus while remaining in small groups in which only one member moves from group to group.

Procedure

1. Divide participants into subgroups of three or four. Ask group members to discuss their views on an impending decision. Encourage them to list specific points of agreement and disagreement.

2. Ask each group to select a reporter. Explain that the reporter's job will be to visit the other small groups and present his or her group's views.

3. Invite reporters to rotate to a group nearby. (If there are only two small groups, the reporters simply exchange seats.) Ask the receiving groups to welcome their "guests."

4. Encourage each group to explain to the reporter after he or she is finished how the views expressed compare to its own.

5. Continue the rotation process until each reporter has visited each small group. When the process is complete, ask the large group whether there appears to be a consensus of views.

85

I Hereby Resolve. . . .

Overview

This is a widely practiced strategy for gaining commitment to the course of action decided at a meeting. It is also an excellent way to help those who have attended the meeting consolidate the various threads of what has been said and add additional weight to the meeting's outcome.

Procedure

1. Ask participants to think about the meeting's accomplishments and what they can commit themselves to do to implement decisions that have been made or to work on an ongoing problem between the present meeting and the next.

2. Provide each participant with a blank sheet of paper and an envelope.

3. Invite participants to write themselves a letter indicating what they (personally) are taking away from the meeting and what steps they intend to take to make the outcome of the meeting successful. Suggest that they begin the letter with the words "I hereby resolve. . . ."

4. Inform the participants that the letters are confidential. Ask each participant to place his or her letter in a self-addressed envelope and to seal it. The letter might sound like this:

   "I hereby resolve to tell everyone affected by this meeting about our deliberations and urge them to support the decisions we have made. I will also do some research before the next meeting on how our constituents feel about the new issues we have raised today."

5. Ask each participant to place a sticky note on the envelope with the date on which he or she wants you to mail the letter. Send the letters to the participants on the dates specified.

Variations

1. Instead of having the participants write to themselves, suggest that they write to someone else who is working on, or at least knows about, the subject of the meeting, indicating their resolve and asking for support.

2. If the project has required a long series of meetings, one month after the last session, send a letter to participants with a summary of the main points accomplished at the meetings. If they are involved in implementing the course of action decided on at the meeting, encourage them to keep in touch with you and offer your expertise to help them solve any unexpected problems.

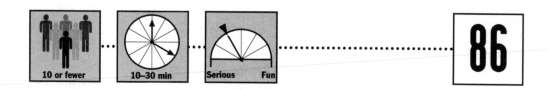

86

I'm Committed*

Overview

Building a level of trust and a willingness by participants to give their best efforts to their organization is growing more and more difficult as downsizing increases and old-fashioned loyalty gives way to skepticism—even among the best workers. This is a good way to attempt to help managers and other employees rebuild their trust or create a new level of dedication toward their companies—or at least their jobs. This exercise would perhaps be most valuable at the beginning of a new sales campaign or a new program of some type that will require extra effort from all employees to be successful.

Procedure

1. Congratulate the group on arriving at a plan of action for a new initiative.

   For example, the project might be the introduction of a company's new global expansion program. The company plans to enter the

---

*Based on a strategy developed by Cathleen Smith Hutchison.

European market by the end of the year and extend its campaign to Asia the following year. The campaign will require new equipment and new training programs, including preparing executives, managers, and the sales force, in order to succeed in the foreign markets; but the company could become the market leader. The project will require a Herculean effort on the part of everyone.

2. Give everyone index cards. Ask participants to think of an occasion when someone they knew (a relative, friend, or co-worker) was highly committed to a certain task. Ask them to think about what they saw that person do and then briefly describe this on the index cards. Then ask them to list the person's main actions and characteristics during that period.

3. Ask individuals to share what they have written, either in the large group or in subgroups if the group is large. Encourage them to discuss the actions and characteristics the person displayed—what they saw the person do that showed his or her dedication to the project. Write a phrase summarizing each person's observations on the flip chart.

4. Ask the group members to find any common elements in the stories. Lead a discussion about the similarities and ask whether there are other ways to show dedication outwardly.

5. Explain to the participants that, although there are common threads to how they show their dedication, people—for whatever reason—often don't show their internal intensity on the surface. A person may be highly committed to a goal but doubtful of its success and so not show his or her feelings; however, a leader will obtain more response from workers if he or she allows the dedication to show through.

6. Point out the major outward ways people judge another person's level of dedication: frequent mention of or action on the issue, a certain excitement or energy level when discussing it, the risk and personal sacrifice the person is willing to make,

and the degree to which he or she feels personally responsible for reaching the goal.

7. Ask the participants if they can add to these ways of judging others' dedication to specific tasks.

8. Ask each participant to write on a piece of paper or index card one or two things he or she can do after the meeting to reinforce what has been accomplished. Suggest that they begin with the phrase: "I am committed to. . . ."

9. Go around the group, asking each person to take a turn reading what he or she has written.

Creating Unforgettable Endings

The End

Meetings should never end with people running out the door before things come to an official end. The close of a meeting should be unforgettable—in two ways: (1) You want the participants to remember vividly what was discussed and to walk away being clear about their follow-up commitments and (2) you also want the meeting to end with a bang, with participants feeling a renewed sense of energy and teamwork. Neither is possible if you don't have techniques to create great meeting closers.

This final section of *101 Ways to Make Meetings Active* contains fifteen strategies to create unforgettable endings. You should find one or two you can use to conclude virtually any meeting or series of meetings. Once your participants become accustomed to memorable meeting closers, they won't want to miss them!

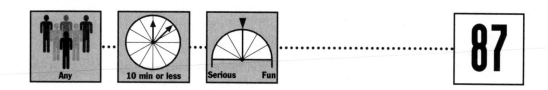

Assessing Obstacles

Overview

Any project that has been planned over a series of meetings should include an assessment of those factors that might interfere with the committee's ability to put into action the ideas they have created and polished. This strategy enables participants to think about and prepare for the obstacles they might face as the concept turns into reality.

Procedure

1. Explain to participants that you hope they will continue to play an active role in the project, even though the planning committee's portion is nearing an end.

2. Ask the participants to predict the obstacles they may have to overcome before the project has been completed. Encourage them to visualize situations in which obstacles may be encountered.

3. Guide the participants in developing positive images of themselves coping with these and other obstacles they may face.

4. Express confidence that participants will be able to access these positive images if the predicted negative scenarios actually unfold.

For example, consider what could happen in a case such as this: The committee has met for months working on plans for a new geriatric wing at a private hospital. Excavation work is about to begin. These are some of the problems they might predict: construction delays due to union disputes; wrong materials ordered, with the correct ones not available for six weeks, causing a monumental problem with subcontractors' schedules; mistakes in the architect's plans; and trouble obtaining final approval on building permits.

In this case, those with construction experience will realize these types of issues occur daily at most construction sites and somehow are always resolved. Their sharing that knowledge with the others will help to ease their anxieties. Together they can consider some "what-if" actions if these or similar problems do indeed occur.

Variation

Instead of using mental imagery, simply ask participants to make a list of obstacles they might face. Suggest that they separate their lists into two headings: "internal" and "external." Internal obstacles refer to attitudes and actions for which participants are personally responsible and may include things like dealing with their own expectations (perhaps they won't like the appearance of the building, even though it does look the way the plans indicated it would). External obstacles refer to attitudes and actions created by other people and events that interfere with one's own resolve. Ask participants to brainstorm ways to overcome both internal and external obstacles.

10–25

10–30 min

Serious   Fun

88

Gallery of Achievement

Overview

This activity is a way to assess and celebrate what participants have been able to accomplish during a series of meetings.

Procedure

1. Divide participants into subgroups of two to four members.

2. Ask each subgroup to discuss what its members are taking away from the meetings. The discussion can cover both personal and professional outcomes. Then ask the subgroups to list their accomplishments on flip-chart paper. Request that they title the list: "What We Have Achieved."

3. Paper the walls with these lists.

4. Ask the participants to walk by each list and to place a check mark next to achievements on lists other than their own that they are taking away as well.

5. Survey the results, noting the most popular accomplishments. Also mention those that are unusual and unexpected. Some examples of comments might be:

- *"We have attained a level of teamwork I didn't think was possible."*
- *"I'm amazed in what an orderly manner the agenda was handled and how quickly the meetings moved."*
- *"We've developed the best possible budget we could. It provides for everything really necessary."*
- *"By coming up with funds to convert the old movie theater into a community center for the arts, we have made possible a program that will bring delight to people of all ages in the community. I'm so proud to have been a part of this committee."*

Variations

1. If the group is small enough, ask each participant to make his or her own list.

2. Instead of listing accomplishments, ask participants to list "keepers"—ideas or suggestions explored during the meetings that are worth keeping or retaining for future use.

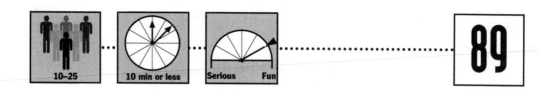

89

Bumper Stickers

Overview

Everyone is familiar with the bumper stickers that often amuse commuters caught in traffic. This strategy enables participants to create their own reminders of meeting accomplishments. These may be signs or lists group members place in or near their work areas or their desks at home to remind them of specific actions to take.

Procedure

1. Invite participants to create "bumper stickers" that express the following:

   - One thing you have learned at the meeting
   - A key thought or piece of advice you will keep in mind to guide you in the future
   - An action step you will take in the future
   - A question to ponder

2. Urge participants to express themselves as concisely as possible. Have them brainstorm possibilities before making their selections. Encourage them to obtain reactions from others.

Some ideas for bumper stickers might be:

- *"Build for the Future"*
- *"I'm the Proud Planner of a Day Care Center"*
- *"Educate a Child, Improve the World"*
- *"Think First, Then Act"*
- *"One Step at a Time, but Make It a Giant One"*

3. Provide materials and supplies so that the participants can make the bumper stickers as attractive as possible.

4. Make a gallery display of the bumper stickers. Make sure participants take theirs with them to display in their work areas.

Variations

1. Make some bumper stickers yourself and give them to participants to take with them.

2. Have participants write bumper sticker ideas on index cards. Gather the cards and pass them around the group. Have each participant select three ideas contributed from other members of the group that will serve him or her well.

90

Follow-Up Questionnaire

Overview

Every newswriter knows that a follow-up story often offers more telling information and a deeper understanding of the issues than the original story. Using that premise as a model, a follow-up questionnaire is a clever strategy for raising participants' consciousness about the meeting subject long after it is over. It also serves as a way to stay in touch with participants.

Procedure

1. Explain to participants that you would like to send them a follow-up questionnaire. The questionnaire is intended (1) to help them remember certain key points addressed during the meetings and (2) to give you feedback.

   For example, consider that you have been chairing an ad hoc committee named by the city to look into some environmental problems concerning city property. These people probably were named to the committee in the first place because they had more than the average citizen's interest in the environment, and it is possible they may even have some new information to be added to the report you are

*preparing. Also, it's possible that these same people will be inter-
ested in other environmental concerns and could be of valuable help
to the city in the future.*

2. Urge the participants to fill out the questionnaire for their
   own benefit and to return the questionnaire only if they so
   desire.

3. When you develop the questionnaire, consider the following
   suggestions:

   • Keep the tone informal and friendly.

   • Arrange the questions so that the easiest to fill out come
     first. Use formats such as checklists, rating scales, incom-
     plete sentences, and short essays.

   • Ask what participants remember the most about the meet-
     ings and what related concerns they are currently pursuing.

   • Offer participants the opportunity to call you with ques-
     tions and other ideas they want to share.

Variations

1. Send follow-up handouts that might be of interest to participants.

2. Instead of sending a questionnaire, interview participants by
   phone or in person. Use a small sample if the number of
   meeting participants was large.

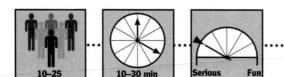

91

Follow-Up Support

Overview

This is a procedure during which participants make a serious commitment to support the efforts of the group now that the meeting(s) is over.

Procedure

1. At the end of your final meeting, ask participants to fill out a statement about the steps they will take to follow up the meeting and support the group's efforts.

   Consider, for example, people who participated in a task force to change the curriculum of an adult education program. They might be asked to complete the following form:

   What steps will you take to ensure that our efforts to revise the curriculum will have been worth the time we put into it?

   1._____

   2._____

   3._____

   4._____

2. Invite participants to share some of their plans publicly. Suggest that people write down any actions suggested by others to which they would be willing to commit themselves as well.

3. When the forms are completed, tell the participants that their statements will be sent to them in three or four weeks to serve as a reminder. At that time, also send these follow-up instructions:

   Please review your follow-up form. Place the letter A next to those actions you have been able to complete. Place the letter B next to those you are still working on. Place the letter C next to those you have not been able to work on.

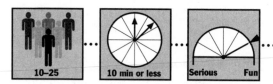

92

Connections

Overview

This is a dramatic and memorable activity that symbolically draws a long series of meetings to a close. It is especially appropriate when participants have formed close connections with one another and offers a visual picture of their accomplishments by using a skein of yarn to literally and symbolically connect participants.

Procedure

1. Bring a skein of yarn to the meeting. Ask everyone to stand and form a circle. Start the process by stating briefly what you have experienced by facilitating the meeting process.

   You might say, for example, that you started out with a roomful of strangers and that you and they, working together, have formed a cohesive and productive organization that has tackled a problem and solved it by connecting with one another.

2. Holding one end of the yarn, toss the skein to a participant on the other side of the circle. Ask that person to state briefly what he or she has experienced as a result of participating in

the meetings. After he or she has spoken, ask that person to hold onto the yarn and toss the skein to another participant.

3. Have each participant take a turn at receiving the skein, sharing reflections, and tossing the yarn again while continuing to hold onto a segment of the yarn. The resulting visual is a web of yarn connecting every member of the group.

   Some samples of what a group of managers from different levels of the organization might say include:

   - *"I learned how important it is to work together as a team."*
   - *"I realize that we all have different personalities and communication styles."*
   - *"I appreciate being given the opportunity to get to know people on a personal level."*
   - *"I feel I can be more open and honest."*
   - *"I know how to deal more effectively with others."*
   - *"I'm going to think of ways to streamline our operation."*

4. Complete the activity by stating that the program began with a collection of individuals willing to connect and work with one another.

5. Cut the yarn with scissors so that each person, though departing as an individual, takes a piece of the other participants with him or her. Thank participants for their interest, ideas, time, and effort.

Variations

1. Ask each participant to express appreciation to the person who tossed the yarn to him or her.

2. Instead of using yarn, toss a ball, a Frisbee®, or a beanbag. As each person receives the tossed object, he or she can express final sentiments.

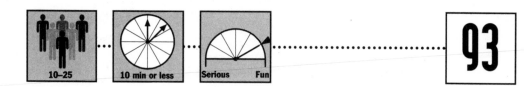

93

10–25   10 min or less   Serious   Fun

Group Photo

Overview

This is an activity that acknowledges the contributions of every participant, while at the same time celebrating the total group.

Procedure

1. Assemble participants for a group photograph. It is best to create at least three rows of participants: one row sitting on the floor, one row sitting in chairs, and one row standing behind the chairs. As you are about to take the picture, express your own final sentiments. Stress how much active meetings depend on the support and involvement of participants. Thank participants for playing such a large part in the success of the entire project.

2. Then invite one participant at a time to leave the group and to be the photographer. (*Optional:* Have each participant merely come up and view what a final picture of the group would look like through the viewfinder.)

3. If the group is not too large, ask each participant to share his or her final thoughts with the others. Ask the group members

to applaud each participant for his or her contributions to the group.

Consider this example: A company founded in 1804 and always tied to the traditional way of conducting business has updated most of its programs and policies over the years, but it wanted to expand its services and offices. It wanted to "jazz up" its public image, while still retaining its historic background and traditional strengths. The company turned this task over to a committee comprising representatives from each business unit, some of whom were up-front about being reluctant to make any changes at all.

Final thoughts as this series of meetings draws to a successful conclusion might include sentiments such as the following:

- *"I thought this might be a waste of time because I thought we'd all only be interested in our own opinions, but I'm really excited about the work we've done together."*

- *"I'm really impressed by the talent I've seen displayed here. We've somehow retained the company's character but moved its image into the 21st Century."*

- *"In the beginning, I wasn't sure we would ever get to the point of listening to one another. By the end, I really trusted everyone."*

4. When the film is developed, send each participant his or her own photograph of the group.

Variations

1. Use the photography session as an opportunity to review some of the highlights of the meetings and any interesting incidents that happened that will keep the joint effort alive in the memories of the participants.

2. Instead of a public disclosure of sentiments, ask participants to write final thoughts on sheets of paper taped to the walls.

94

What? So What? Now What?

Overview

The value of any meeting is enhanced by asking participants to reflect on the experience they just had and to explore its implications. This reflection period is often referred to as "processing" or "debriefing." Here is a three-stage sequence for processing or debriefing a meeting. Avoid the temptation to ask all these questions simultaneously.

Procedure

1. Ask participants to share **what** happened to them during the meeting:

   • *"What did you do?"*

   • *"What did you observe? Think about?"*

   • *"What feelings did you have during the meeting?"*

   You may also use any of the options listed in "Ten Methods for Obtaining Group Participation" on page 17 to obtain responses.

2. Next ask participants to ask themselves: **"So what?"**

- *"What benefits did you gain from the meeting?"*

- *"What did you learn? Relearn?"*

- *"What are the implications of the meeting for the whole group's efforts?"*

3. Finally, ask participants to consider implications: **"Now what?"**

    - *"How do you want to do things differently in the future?"*

    - *"How can you extend the meeting experience you had?"*

    - *"What steps can you take to support what has been accomplished?"*

95

How Did We Do?

Overview

A public process of sharing reactions to the meeting process creates a sense that "We're all in this together." There are a variety of ways to design the group's assessment of its work together and answer the question: "How did we do?" Here are some options.

Procedure

1. Hand out a list of specific questions to evaluate the meeting. Some concrete questions you can ask include the following:

   - *"Did the meetings start on time?"*
   - *"Were the necessary people there?"*
   - *"Did the meetings stay on course?"*
   - *"Was the leader flexible enough?"*
   - *"Was time to speak distributed fairly?"*
   - *"Were opinions listened to?"*
   - *"Were deadlines and assignments clearly defined?"*
   - *"Would you consider the meetings successful?"*

- *"Was the mission of the meetings achieved?"*
- *"What could have been done differently?"*

Set aside 5 to 10 minutes for open discussion. Participants can freely choose any question to answer.

2. Or consider obtaining feedback from participants by distributing a short post-meeting reaction form. Confine the questions to your goals and concerns. Leave off the participants' names so they can be totally honest. Promise to report the results in summary form.

A post-meeting reaction form might look like this:

Please evaluate our meetings by circling the number that best describes your reaction to each pair of words.

1	2	3	4	5
Unproductive				**Productive**

1	2	3	4	5
Fragmented				**Cohesive**

1	2	3	4	5
Frustrating				**Satisfying**

1	2	3	4	5
Tense				**Relaxed**

1	2	3	4	5
Unfinished agenda				**Completed agenda**

3. Consider a feedback form in which participants complete sentence stems, such as the following:

I came expecting. . . .

I experienced. . . .

Next time, I hope we. . . .

4. Or ask participants to discuss their reactions to any of these general questions:

- *"Was this meeting worth the investment of our collective time and energy?"*

- *"What happened at this meeting that was **helpful? Not helpful?**"*

- *"Using **hindsight,** how could this meeting have been improved?"*

- *"For the next time we meet, what should we **stop doing, start doing, continue doing?**"*

Remember to use a discussion format that suits your situation the best. Calling on the next speaker may be a very appropriate method here.

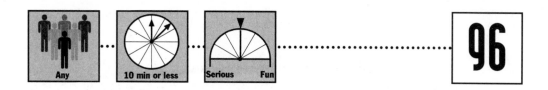

Thank You

Overview

When members of a committee have spent hours together working on a specific project, there definitely will be a need, expressed or not, to thank one another and to give themselves a little pat on the back. You can help them achieve this happy ending by providing a way for them to celebrate the group's work and to keep in touch in the future, if they wish.

Procedure

1. You will need to take to the meeting one envelope (large enough to hold several index cards) per participant and several index cards per person. Also provide pens and postage stamps, if you wish.

2. If the group is large, divide it into subgroups of six or eight. This activity will also work for a single group of up to ten people.

3. Give each person an envelope and enough index cards to be passed to others in the group. For example, if the group is made up of six people, give each person five index cards.

4. Ask each participant to write his or her name on the address side of the envelope and then pass the envelope to the person on his or her right.

5. Tell people to read the name on the envelope just received and to complete the following sentence stem on one of the index cards—in reference to the person whose name is on the envelope:

    • Thank you for. . . .

6. Tell participants to place the cards in the envelopes and pass them to the person on their right. As they receive new envelopes, ask them *not* to read the cards written by others, but to fill out a new card for the person whose name is on the new envelope.

7. Continue the process until all the cards have been used and each of the envelopes has been returned to the person whose name is on it.

8. Give each person the choice either to read his or her notes immediately or to read them later in private.

Variation

Send each participant a personal thank-you note expressing your gratitude to each for his or her participation in the work of the committee or board. Some thanks you might want to express include:

• *"Thank you for pitching in to support my idea."*
• *"Thanks for your positive attitude throughout the meetings."*
• *"I really appreciated your honesty and your integrity."*
• *"Your common sense came to the rescue many times and carried us through some difficult decisions."*

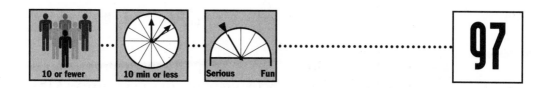

Are We on the Same Page?

Overview

It's essential to confirm that everyone has a similar understanding of the status of every agenda item either before or soon after a meeting has ended. It's also imperative to confirm any follow-up activities needed: "Who will do what by when?" Here are some options to find out whether everyone is "on the same page."

Procedure

1. Ask the participants to go around the group, with each person stating his or her understanding of the major decisions made and the next steps for items that are either unfinished or must be confirmed. A participant may also use his or her turn to confirm the understanding of other participants.

2. Or summarize the meeting outcome yourself, including what actions were taken and the outcome of each action. You might also consider designating in advance a person other than the traditional minute-taker to provide such a summary. Then, ask participants whether the summary is accurate.

3. Or—after the meeting is over—prepare an executive summary that documents the achievements of the group and the business that is unfinished. Urge participants to contact you and another designated person if they have a different understanding on any point. Don't leave discrepancies to be corrected until minutes are up for approval at the next meeting. By then, it's too late.

4. Most important of all, check that any follow-up activity is clearly understood. List what actions the group has agreed to, who is responsible for doing them, and by when they are to be completed.

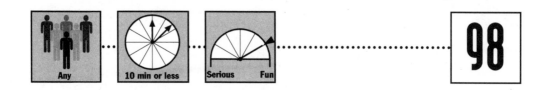

Ballooning Messages

Overview

Here is a fun way to end a meeting in which participants express their final thoughts to one another in an anonymous and creative fashion.

Procedure

1. Bring to the meeting a bag of balloons of various colors and distribute one to each participant. Also, give each person a small piece of paper that can be inserted into a balloon.

2. Ask each participant to write a message on the small piece of paper. Compare it to the insert in a Chinese fortune cookie. Some suggested message topics could be:

   - *My reaction to today's meeting*
   - *Something I promise to do before the next meeting*
   - *Something or someone I appreciated*
   - *A reason why the meeting was productive/unproductive*
   - *A question that remains from today's meeting*

3. Have each participant insert his or her message in a balloon, blow it up, and then tie it. At a common signal, have participants place their balloons into a large container, such as an oversized trash bag.

4. Give out one balloon randomly to each participant. Invite the participants to pop their balloons and find the inserted messages.

5. Have participants read aloud the message they received.

Variation

Instead of using balloons, give each participant a standard piece of paper. Have him or her write a message on the paper and crumple it up into a ball or simply fold it in half. Collect the papers and distribute them around the group.

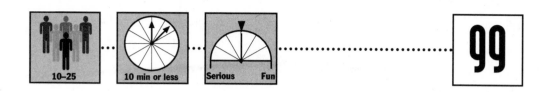

99

When the Spirit Moves You

Overview

Final thoughts to wrap up a meeting can also be expressed in the form of a Quaker meeting. Members of the Society of Friends speak up "when the spirit moves them," and this is a good method for participants to follow.

Procedure

1. Explain to participants that Quakers are accustomed to expressing themselves without being called on. Instead, they wait until the "spirit moves them" and then speak up. Indicate that you would like to end the meeting in a similar fashion.

2. Provide a list of sentence stems that participants can use to express their final sentiments "when the spirit moves them." Here are some possibilities:

   - *I felt that the meeting. . . .*
   - *Something I'm excited about is. . . .*
   - *At our next meeting, I would like us to. . . .*

- *A concern I have leaving this meeting is. . . .*
- *I want to thank. . . .*
- *One thing I liked about the way we worked together is. . . .*
- *I wish we. . . .*
- *Something I'm going to do tomorrow is. . . .*

3. Begin the activity by inviting people to share their completions to the sentence stems you have chosen. Encourage them not to respond to what others say before them, but to use the Quaker meeting style. Start by saying: "Who wants to begin?" Wait through the silence until someone's spirit is moved to start the process.

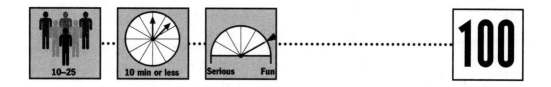

100

10–25   10 min or less   Serious   Fun

Down the Lane*

Overview

This is a meeting closer that you can use whenever it is appropriate for people to congratulate one another or say goodbye in a public manner.

Procedure

1. Have the participants form two straight lines facing each other with a space in between. Refer to this space between lines as the "lane."

2. Ask the two people at the head of the lines to enter the lane and to walk single file down it. Encourage people in the lines to give them pats on the back, hand shakes, high-fives, hugs, or whatever seems an appropriate way to say goodbye and acknowledge their contributions to the meeting.

3. When the first two people finish going down the lane, they join the end of the line on either side, and the next two peo-

*Based on a strategy developed by Sharon Bowman.

ple at the head of the line proceed through the lane, and so on until everyone has gone through the lane.

Variations

1. Form one long line. Stand at the beginning of the line and walk along in front of each person, shaking hands or whatever seems appropriate. Join the end of the line. Each subsequent person does the same until everyone has had a turn.

2. Form two concentric circles of equal numbers of participants. Ask the people in the inner circle to face those in the outer circle. The outer circle people move to the right when they are told to rotate and exchange handshakes or other forms of goodbye with each inner circle person.

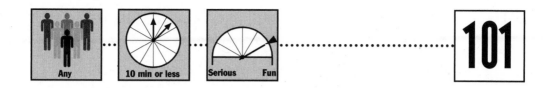

101

Meeting "Rap-Up"*

Overview

If you don't mind the play on words, why not wrap up the meeting with rap songs. It's an activity that is infectious and fun.

Procedure

1. Explain that you would like to "wrap up" the meeting by having everyone "rap" about it.

2. Divide participants into small groups of two to four members. Give them the beginning lines for a rap song they will create and perform in front of the entire group. Encourage them to use a syncopated beat. Here are some possible opening lines:

   - *The meeting is done,*
     It sure was. . . .

   - *Now, it's time,*
     To say goodbye. . . .

---

*Based on a strategy developed by Rebecca Birch and Cynthia Denton-Ade.

- *Our group is great,*
  Our. . . .

- *In closing our meeting,*
  We'd like to say. . . .

3. Provide 5 minutes for each group to compose its rap song. Here is an example of a completed rap:

The meeting is done,
It sure was fine,
Time to celebrate it,
With some fine wine.
How good it is,
To be able to shine,
With friends so smart,
And friends so fine.
Yeh, Yeh, Yeh, Yeh!

4. Invite each group to perform its rap and encourage everyone else to repeat it. Enjoy the celebration of hard work. That's what active meetings are all about!

Further Reading

I have found these books to be terrific resources for meeting facilitators.

Butler, A. (1996). *The trainer's guide to running effective meetings.* New York: McGraw-Hill.

Chang, R., & Kehoe, K. (1994). *Meetings that work!* Irvine, CA: Richard Chang.

Kelsey, D., & Plumb, P. (1998). *Great meetings! How to facilitate like a pro.* Portland, ME: Hansom Park Press.

Lawson, K. (1999). *Involving your audience: Making it active.* Needham Heights, MA: Allyn & Bacon.

Logson, T. (1993). *Breaking through.* Reading, MA: Addison-Wesley.

Mattimore, B. (1994). *99 percent inspiration.* New York: AMACOM.

Mosvick, R., & Nelson, R. (1996). *We've got to start meeting like this!* Indianapolis, IN: Park Avenue.

Napier, R., & Gershenfeld, M. (1983). *Making groups work: A guide for group leaders.* Boston, MA: Houghton-Mifflin.

Rees, F. (1991). *How to lead work teams.* San Francisco, CA: Jossey-Bass/Pfeiffer.

Schwarz, R. (1994). *The skilled facilitator.* San Francisco, CA: Jossey-Bass.

Ury, W. (1993). *Getting past no: Negotiating your way from confrontation to cooperation.* New York: Bantam.

Weisbord, M., & Janoff, S. (1995). *Future search.* San Francisco, CA: Berrett-Koehler.

About the Authors

Mel Silberman, Ph.D., is president of Active Training, a provider of cutting-edge training seminars, including *Surefire Ways to Make Your Meeting Active* and *The Consummate Team Facilitator*. He can be contacted at the following address:

Active Training
26 Linden Lane
Princeton, NJ 08540
800-924-8157
mel@activetraining.com
Or visit his website at *www.activetraining.com*

Dr. Silberman is also professor of adult and organizational development at Temple University and a best-selling author. His recent books include *101 Ways to Make Training Active* (Jossey-Bass/Pfeiffer, 1995), *Active Learning* (Allyn & Bacon, 1996), *Active Training* (2nd ed.) (Jossey-Bass/Pfeiffer, 1998).

He is also editor of *20 Active Training Programs, Vols. 1, 2,* and *3* (Jossey-Bass/Pfeiffer, 1992, 1994, & 1997); *The Team and Organization Development Sourcebook* (McGraw-Hill, 1996–1999); and *The Training and Performance Sourcebook* (McGraw-Hill, 1996–1999).

Dr. Silberman has consulted for hundreds of corporate, governmental, educational, and human service organizations worldwide. He is also a popular speaker at professional conferences.

Kathy Clark assisted with *101 Ways to Make Meetings Active*. Ms. Clark is senior editor of *Human Resource Executive*, a leading trade magazine on strategic HR issues published by LRP Publications, Inc., Horsham, PA. Ms. Clark is responsible for the magazine's coverage of trends in training and development, diversity issues, and telecommuting. She is a graduate of Barnard College, Columbia University. She can be reached at *Kfc17@aol.com.*